Tales from the

WEST MIDLANDS
◄►◄ CANALS ►◄►

Tales from the
WEST MIDLANDS
•◆• CANALS •◆•

R.H. Davies

First published 2010

The History Press
The Mill, Brimscombe Port
Stroud, Gloucestershire, GL5 2QG
www.thehistorypress.co.uk

British Library Cataloguing in Publication Data.
A catalogue record for this book is available from the British Library.

ISBN 978 0 7524 5500 6

Typesetting and origination by The History Press
Printed in Great Britain

CONTENTS

INTRODUCTION AND
ACKNOWLEDGEMENTS

This book is essentially a journey through 200 years of canal history. We commence with the prime movers of the canal schemes of the late eighteenth century, that is to say the members of the Lunar Society of Birmingham, and conclude with more recent events. Many of us are familiar with the famous names of the designers and builders of the canal network, but who were its motivators? They included such influential people as Erasmus Darwin, Charles Darwin's grandfather, Matthew Boulton, the early Birmingham

Pitstone Church on the Grand Union Canal near Berkhamsted, where William Perry went to get married with his young bride who claimed to be twenty-one when in fact she was still only seventeen.

industrialist, and James Watt, his partner in steam. Others, such as Josiah Wedgwood, had just as significant a share in promoting the waterways that we enjoy today.

In more recent years, I have been fortunate enough to interview some extremely interesting boatmen and women who worked the waterways during and after the Second World War. Their numbers are dwindling all the time, but they played an important role in their time and have their own story to tell.

Fortunately they have allowed me to gently tap into their memories and use their photographs, and for this I thank them all, along with members of the local canal societies who also undertake fine work. My thanks go also to members of the Birmingham Canal Navigations Society (BCNS) for their friendly support; to Keith Hodgkins of the Tipton Civic Society; to my wife Jane for genealogical work, and to Ray Shill for help with the slasher research. If there are any mistakes – and there always are in any book – then I humbly apologise.

2008 was a very busy year for boating activity around the Birmingham Canal Navigations (BCN). There was the Inland Waterways Association (IWA) national at Wolverhampton, the new Tipton festival, the Dudley Canal Celebrations, including the 150th anniversary of the opening of the Netherton Tunnel, a gathering of historic boats at Parkhead, Dudley, a BCNS cruise and, finally, a later gathering at Stourbridge. I have tried to cover at least some of that ground.

Tipton is certainly known for two things; one is its canals, the other is the legendary pugilist from the 1850s – The Tipton Slasher – William Perry. The slasher material in this book is entirely new research. Some of you may know that I wrote a short biography of the Tipton Slasher in 2008. Rather ironically, as soon as that book was published by The Wednesbury Book Shop, I discovered a whole host of new information about him, information which now lies within the cover of this book.

Every effort has been made to ensure that all material is accurately credited where necessary. Where any acknowledgements have been inadvertently missed, please accept my apologies.

R.H. Davies

1

THE LUNAR SOCIETY

Occasionally historians will debate the question – why did the industrial revolution take place in Britain and not elsewhere? The discussion will take note of certain inventions, the availability of capital, entrepreneurialism and all kinds of other forces, even the fact that Britain was a nation of tea drinkers – which helped to keep its workforce healthy. The truth is there were many contributing factors, but a very important one was the gathering of men (sorry girls but it was nearly all men) into groups that had a great zeal for knowledge and advancement. One group that probably had more influence on the change from an agriculturally based world to an industrial one – and especially that of canals – was The Lunar Society. But just who were they?

The Lunar Society was a group of individuals who became firm friends. The group included James Watt, of steam engine fame; Matthew Boulton, one of the first men to operate a modern-style factory; Josiah Wedgwood, the potter; James Keir, the Tipton chemist; Erasmus Darwin, doctor and inventor from Lichfield; Joseph Priestly; Samuel Galton; Dr William Small; William Withering, and a few others such as Thomas Day and Richard Lovell Edgeworth. These men met and corresponded for friendship, advancement and a love of knowledge. They came to be called the Lunatics by Samuel Galton's butler, because it was their custom to travel and meet at night by a full moon – no street lights in those days, you see!

Some of the names will be instantly recognisable from your school history lessons, others are less well known. How do we start to describe them? Well, they were doctors, engineers, businessmen, scientists and even clergymen, but they were also family men, and above all else they were friends. Friends who loved to talk, to share a meal and laughter together, and of course to encourage each other in whatever endeavour they were involved in at that moment. There were no mobile phones in those days and they kept in touch via letters, of which they wrote hundreds between them. Fortunately – for history and for us – much of that fascinating correspondence has been preserved. It was this exchange of information, the men meeting on full moons, the passing on of knowledge, the web of contacts that they had, which moved the world forward.

They lived in the second half of the eighteenth century, a period of great social change. This was, of course, the time when cities were growing, when the factory emerged, and when there was a general move by people away from the countryside and into the towns looking for work. It was the time of the French Revolution, and of the war when the American colonies broke away from British rule. It was also the time when the industrial canal made its first appearance, and these men were instrumental in the promotion of Britain's industrial canal system.

Each man is worthy of study in his own right. There is James Watt, with his amazing steam engine, and Joseph Priestly, who discovered oxygen. Perhaps the most intriguing of the group, however, was the overweight and stammering genius, Dr Erasmus Darwin. Certainly the name Darwin rings a bell. Indeed one automatically thinks of Charles Darwin of evolution fame, but it was his grandfather, Erasmus, who was the real originator of the theory – Charles only picked up the baton, so to speak. Yes, it was Erasmus who came up with the theory that all things originated from simpler life forms, and it all started when the Harecastle Tunnel was dug on the Trent & Mersey Canal. But first, a small sketch of Erasmus, from a lady who knew him well:

> What then was my astonishment at beholding him as he slowly got out of the carriage? His figure was vast and massive, his head was almost buried in his shoulders, and he wore a scratch wig as it was then called, tied up in a little bobtail behind. A habit of stammering made the closest attention necessary, in order to understand what he said. Meanwhile, amidst all this, the doctor's eye was deeply sagacious – his observation was most keen; he constantly detected disease from his sagacious observation of symptoms apparently so slight as to be unobserved by other doctors.

Certainly Erasmus was more than a doctor, for he was constantly designing and redesigning parts for his horse-drawn carriage – he invented the type of steering that we use on the car today. Now, to return to the Harecastle tunnel and the evolution theory.

When the navvies were digging the Harecastle Tunnel during the 1760s they came across all kinds of things. At the time there was much interest in the age of the earth, and many peopel – including the Lunar members – collected rocks and minerals. So it was no surprise that, when large animal remains were found under a bed of clay, they were sent to Darwin for examination and, hopefully, identification. Of course the doctor was at a loss as to what they were; and in a letter to Wedgwood he wrote, 'The bone seems to be the third vertebra of the back of a camel. The horn is larger than any modern horn I have measured, and must be that of a Patagonian ox'. Darwin was, of course, talking through his hat, and Wedgwood knew it

However, as the years rolled by it was Erasmus who developed the theory of evolution, though it was much too early for such an anti-God scheme to be published. Erasmus lived under the shadow of Lichfield Cathedral, and realising that he would cause a great deal of trouble if he took on the religious establishment at that time, he backed away from that potential confrontation. In recent years many have come down on the side of design and creationism, and the debate is still ongoing.

Lichfield Cathedral. Lichfield was the cultural centre of the Midlands during the eighteenth century. Erasmus Darwin, doctor, inventor and poet, lived here for much of his life and his house was much visited by other members of the Lunar Society.

Rear of Darwin's House (left), Lichfield.

JAMES KIER

James Keir was born in Scotland in 1735. Like some of the other Lunar men, he started out studying medicine, going to Edinburgh to study. The world of academia failed to provide the excitement that he craved in his youth, so he joined the army and went overseas. When he had got this wanderlust out of his system, he came back to England and settled in Stourbridge, working in the glass trade, rather an unusual progression one might think!

It was here that he started his experiments in chemistry, as well as corresponding with his old friend, Watt. Other associates included Dr Black, Dr Small, who was responsible for introducing many of the Lunar men to each other, and Benjamin Franklin who we know as the man who – by dangerous means – invented the lightning conductor.

Chemistry seemed to be the area that grabbed Keir's interest, and he abandoned glass making for the production of alkali at a new works in Tipton – right next to the Birmingham Canal. He went on to make much of his money from soap, no less. Keir was known to be well mannered and witty in society, just in his dealings with others, and wise and practical in his giving of advice. The Tipton factory was regarded by contemporaries as a technological marvel, second only to that of Boulton's in Soho, and was powered by water and steam. To supply his works with coal, Keir and partners sank a mine in Tividale in 1794, and today you will find Keir's Bridge over the old main line as a reminder of the clever Mr Keir.

Soho House, Birmingham, the home of Matthew Boulton. It is now a visitor centre.

The dining room at Soho. The group must have spent much time here, eating and talking.

MATTHEW BOULTON

Matthew Boulton, with a father of the same name, grew up in the expanding world of Birmingham industry during the early eighteenth century, where his father made metal fancy goods, known then as 'toys'. Many of our Lunar men were not opposed to making money, and Birmingham was quickly becoming the place to make one's fortune. The early factory was in Slaney Street at Snow Hill, where Matthew Junior was born in a house behind the workshop. Young Matthew grew up and, after living at Sarehole Mill for a while, he moved his manufacturing interests to a place at Soho in Handsworth.

Four years previously this site had been developed by a John Taylor as a rolling mill. Its useful position, only a mile and a half from the centre of Birmingham, was advantageous in having the Hockley Brook to provide power to a waterwheel. The buildings he developed became known as the Soho Manufactory, not to be confused with the Soho Foundry which was built much later, a mile away in Smethwick. At the Soho Manufactory, Boulton made a large array of metal goods and came to employ over seven hundred workers and artisans, supplying a global market. He was a caring employer who gave serious and practical attention to improving the lot of his workers by such means as providing accommodation, whitewashing the interior of buildings for cleanliness and light, and operating an insurance scheme for those that became sick.

But Boulton required power. The Hockley Brook drove a 20ft overshot waterwheel, which soon became woefully inadequate for supplying the power to Soho machinery. When Boulton heard about James Watt and his ideas for the improving of the steam engine, Boulton instinctively recognised that this was the answer to his, and to others', problems. They quickly became firm, lifelong friends, and Boulton invited Watt to Birmingham permanently. He wrote to Watt in 1769:

> ... my idea was to settle a manufactory near to my own by the side of our canal, where I would erect all the conveniences necessary for the completion of the engines, and from which manufactory we would serve all the world with engines of all sizes. By these means and your assistance we could engage and instruct some excellent workmen (with more excellent tools than would be worth any mans while to procure for one single engine) and could execute the invention 20 per cent cheaper than it would be otherwise executed, and with a difference of accuracy as there is between the blacksmith and the mathematical instrument maker. It would not be worth my while to make for three counties only; but I find it well worth my while to make for all the world.

Watt's genius lay not in the invention of the steam engine, as some erroneously believe, but in its improvement, and he went on to develop its design, increase its efficiency, and to adapt it to turn geared wheels. The move to rotary motion was the breakthrough that manufacturers keenly desired. It meant that they could scrap their waterwheels and turn their machinery with greater power and constancy. This led to Boulton's famous saying, 'I sell here, Sir, what all the world desires to have – Power'. Boulton's plan was to construct many of the parts for the new steam engine at one site, and that is where the Soho Foundry came in.

Before Watt met Boulton, however, he worked for some time as the surveyor of several canal schemes. It was with his Birmingham partner, Matthew Boulton, that he recognised that the Birmingham Canal was the perfect transport technology for their new venture. So they constructed the first factory to produce steam engines right alongside the Brindley waterway. Boulton and Watt steam engines, when developed in the last quarter of the 1700s, became extremely important in keeping many of the BCN waterways active. They were the great pumping engines that recycled the millions of gallons of water lost down the locks.

THE SOHO FOUNDRY

Negotiations for the purchase of land next to the winding Birmingham Canal at Smethwick began in the middle of 1795, and within a short time building had begun. Watt's son, James Watt Junior (who effectively took over the business after the death of his father in 1819), wrote on 14 September 1795 that '... the new buildings are going on at full gallop and hope to have the brickwork completed this week'.

One month later, two buildings had been roofed, while two more were in the process of receiving theirs. The foundry measured 100ft by 70ft. Then, in 1796, there were great celebrations and feasting for the workmen and smiths as the site officially opened.

Above left: Site of the Soho Foundry, Birmingham Main Line Canal, Smethwick.

Above right: Statue of Boulton, Watt and Murdock in Birmingham.

Part of the old Soho Foundry.

Galton Bridge, Smethwick.

Two fat sheep (the first fruits of the newly cultivated land at Soho) were sacrificed on the Altar of Vulcan and eaten by the Cyclops in the Great Hall of the Temple, which is 46 wide by 100 feet long. These two great dishes were garnished with rumps and rounds of beef, legs of veal, and gammons of bacon with innumerable meat pies and plum puddings, accompanied with a good band of martial music. When dinner was over, the founder of Soho [Boulton] entered and consecrated the new branch by sprinkling the walls with wine, and then in the name of Vulcan, and all the gods and goddesses of fire and water, pronounced the name of it – Soho Foundry – and all the people cried 'Amen', such was the enthusiasm and pseudo religious fervour for the new enterprise.[1]

Boulton then went on to praise his workers by saying, 'As the Smith cannot do without his striker, so neither can the master do without his workmen,' and concluded by remarking that the buildings had been erected in a short time when one considered the inclement season, and that no one had lost their life in the grand undertaking.

And so the Soho Foundry commenced the manufacture of steam engines, not only for Britain's canal system and industries but, as Boulton had predicted, for 'the whole world'.

1 Dickinson, Henry Winram (1937), *Matthew Boulton*, pp 168–169.

JOSIAH WEDGWOOD

Interestingly, in *Canals of the West Midlands* by Charles Hadfield, the modern-day bible of the Midland canals, he starts with an imaginary conversation between Wedgwood and Darwin:

> About February 1756, we may imagine a meeting between Dr Erasmus Darwin of Lichfield, physician, scientist and poet, then a man of thirty three, and Josiah Wedgwood, potter of Burslem, then thirty four, and for the last six years the master of his own business. Wedgwood probably talked on his favourite subject of the transport difficulties of himself and his fellow potters.

In essence, the potter's wares were being transported to various points around the country, mainly on horseback, a risky and costly business as many were broken in transit. Darwin listened to Wedgwood's just complaints, reminded him of the work that Brindley had already done with his canals up north, and suggested that this Brindley may be the man to consult.

As soon as the Trent & Mersey Canal was planned, Darwin fancied himself a bit of a businessman too. Creating a partnership with Samuel Garbett, the paper-maker John Bage, and a local banker John Barker, they planned to construct a short section of canal a little to the north-east of Lichfield.

The canal would provide a water source to power an iron rolling and slitting mill, and then later on, when the Trent & Mersey Canal came along, they could sell their little section to the canal company. The idea was a good one, though unfortunately it did not do too well financially: but Darwin was not to be put off canals. He was wise and practical enough to see which way the wind was blowing.

Josiah Wedgwood was a man that came to be loved and admired by his own generation. Today, Wedgwood is an inspirational model for anyone who wants to triumph over adversity and continually strive for improvement. Indeed, Wedgwood hauled himself up from a humble and painful childhood to set fine standards in the field of pottery, to genuinely care about the welfare of others, and en route he became one of the most important promoters for Britain's canals.

What then were his beginnings? What sort of privations did he suffer? And how did he become intimately connected with James Brindley, the Duke of Bridgewater, and other people of significance who gave so much impetus to the industrial revolution? First, we need to understand the kind of conditions around Burslem when Josiah was a boy.

Josiah was born in 1730, the youngest of thirteen children. He entered an environment that could be called a dynasty of potters, though it must be said on a small scale. His father, Thomas Wedgwood, was one of almost a clan of Wedgwoods living in Staffordshire. He had a small works known as the Churchyard Pottery in Burslem, near

Stoke on Trent, where he employed about six men. However, this was not the refined pottery that went into the fine houses of the day. At Burslem they turned out such common household items as soup and porridge dishes as well as other kitchenware.

At the age of seven, Josiah went to a small informal school kept by a Mr Blunt to learn his elementary ABCs. He was not there long, however, for his father died when he was just nine years old. Fortunately he possessed that inner motivation that drove him to essentially educate himself. Books were the means to knowledge for Josiah, as they were for others who had a hunger for information and wanted to improve their lot in life.

For two years he became occupied at what was now his brother's pottery works, and young Josiah had a gift and love for making clay models. His older brother was, apparently, unimpressed with his early artistic prowess. However, at the age of only eleven, his endurance was to be severely tested.

SMALLPOX IN BURSLEM

In 1741 there was an outbreak of smallpox in Burslem, and Josiah, along with many others, became extremely ill. For a long period the boy was not strong enough to get out of bed, and though he did eventually recover, his convalescence took many months and his health was never the same. At length he got up and used crutches, but the virus had permanently damaged his knee, and he would get continual pain from this, as well as trouble with his eyesight throughout his life. In fact, after an accident much later in life he was in so much pain that he actually had his leg amputated without the benefit of any anaesthetic.

However, as a lad he eventually went back to throwing pots and became quite skilful, entering into an apprenticeship. At the age of twenty he inherited £20, and while not a tremendous fortune it at least gave him a start. As the years went by, Josiah had a succession of partnerships and his business grew steadily. To understand how he came to be heavily involved with the planning and building of the inland waterway system, we need to understand what conditions were like in Burslem during the first half of the eighteenth century.

STAFFORDSHIRE TRANSPORT

The Staffordshire of that time had a shortage of roads, and those that did exist were rough dirt bridleways, full of rocks and puddles. The landlocked situation of the potters at Burslem was worse than inconvenient, and though much of the clay was close at hand, the only way to get their pots to market was on the back of the pack horses that lumbered and stumbled along the track ways. The poor horses, urged on by the lash, stumbled through the mud and often fell, upsetting their small loads and causing many breakages. If the horse broke a leg, he was often shot where he fell.

Erasmus Darwin.

Matthew Boulton.

To correct this intolerable situation, Josiah attempted to improve the road system, but there were many people that objected. New roads did not suit the needs of everyone. Josiah's main transport objective was to reach the port of Liverpool on the west coast. The busy port served not only Britain, but America too, while the port of Hull on the east coast would serve interests in Europe. There had to be a better way of getting his valuable yet fragile goods to these two ports.

The idea of a navigation between these two towns had already been much talked about. The Duke of Bridgewater had after all just built his Worsley to Manchester Canal in 1761. Wedgwood had known James Brindley for some time, as Brindley had been involved in building a mill for the grinding of flint in Staffordshire. However, the construction of a canal of such length, and across such difficult terrain, was an enormous undertaking. But Wedgwood knew that if anyone could accomplish this waterway, Brindley could. He was already known as 'The Schemer' and had constructed what, for that day, was an amazing feat – an aqueduct over the River Irwell that had been nicknamed 'The Castle in the Air'.

RELATIONSHIP WITH THE DUKE OF BRIDGEWATER.

Wedgwood came to have such a close association with the Duke of Bridgewater that he wrote on 6 July 1765:

> I have been waiting upon his Grace the Duke of Bridgewater with plans respecting inland navigation. Mr Sparrow went along with me. We were most graciously received; we spent about eight hours in his Grace's company and had all the assurances of his concurrence in our designs that we could wish. His Grace gave me an order for the complete set of table service of cream-colour that I could make. He showed us a Roman urn, 1500 years old at least, made of red china, which had been found by his workmen in Castle Field near Manchester. After his Grace had dismissed us we had the honour and pleasure of sailing on his gondola some nine miles along his canal, through a most delightful vale to Manchester.

The first public movement in support of Brindley's survey occurred in December 1765, when an open-air meeting was held at Wolsley Bridge. Attending were big names including Earl Gower, Lord Grey, Mr Bagot, Mr Anson, Mr Gilbert and, of course, Wedgwood and Brindley. The plans were fully discussed and adopted, and it was resolved to obtain the necessary Act of Parliament. Wedgwood, with his usual generosity, subscribed £1,000 towards the preliminary expenses and also promised to subscribe for a sizeable proportion of the shares.

The main promoters of the scheme were originally going to name it 'The Canal from the Trent to the Mersey', but Brindley knew that this canal would be only the start of a much larger project, one that would eventually connect up with other waterways, and he wisely suggested that they call it 'The Grand Trunk'.

WAR OF THE PAMPHLETS

The Staffordshire potters were delighted with the plans, and the following day they had a bonfire at Burslem where they drank the health of the promoters. However, just as there had been opponents to the road schemes, there were many who bitterly objected to the canal proposals, especially the owners of the Weaver Navigation, who did not want to lose the great advantage they already enjoyed. Both sides went to war, with pamphlets as their weapon of choice. Wedgwood's was entitled *A view of the advantages of inland navigations: with a plan of a navigable canal, intended for a communication between the ports of Liverpool and Hull.*

The promoters had a battle of the pamphlets on their hands. Nevertheless, they knew that the real difficulty was going to be getting the waterway over, or through, the high ground at Harecastle. This was where Brindley's confidence and natural zeal shone through. The battle of the pamphlets developed into tough verbal exchanges in Parliament, but the promoters had some big guns on their side, and eventually the project went through on 14 May 1766.

There were more rejoicings at Burslem, and the first sod was dug by Wedgwood on 26 July that summer. Wedgwood's leg was so bad at that time that Brindley barrowed the earth away amidst loud cheers. At a meeting of the proprietors, Wedgwood was appointed treasurer, demonstrating the esteem that he was held in. Brindley's salary was fixed at £200 per annum, but Wedgwood was worried about his friend for he wrote to another close companion, Mr Bentley, in March 1767:

> I am afraid Brindley is endeavouring to do too much, and that he will leave us before his vast designs are accomplished. He is so incessantly harassed on every side that he hath no rest for either mind or body, and he will not be prevailed upon to take proper care of his health.

Later in March he wrote again on a similar subject. His admiration for Brindley was great, but he also recognised that the man was only going to fall into an early grave if he continued with such a punishing work schedule.

At one of the first committee meetings, the newly formed canal company ordered that work should start at both ends of the proposed Harecastle Tunnel – a project that was not to be finished for eleven years. Yet, through all those years, Wedgwood stuck firmly to his resolve in order that the problems for the potters of Staffordshire would finally be solved. In the meanwhile he built his famous works of Etruria right on the banks of the new canal, ensuring that raw materials could be boated in from as far away as Cornwall, and that finished goods could reach the rest of the world.

2

THE LORDS OF DUDLEY

The early industrial years brought a harsh life to thousands as they toiled in the mines, quarries and factories that came to fill the landscape of the Midlands. They were the workers at the base of an economic triangle, while at the apex a small group of privileged people lived a most luxurious lifestyle. The Earls of Dudley came to be among that celebrated number.

Their wealth came from leased agricultural estates and from the subterranean stores of coal, iron ore, limestone and clays. They owned and rented many of the mines, iron works and some of the canals of the Black Country. Witley Court – a magnificent Italian-style mansion, close to the town of Stourport – was the prize for much of that industrial output. While miners, boatmen, foundry workers and their families survived on just the basics of existence, ladies attending a Christmas gathering at Witley were invited to take gifts of expensive jewels from the Christmas tree.

At the end of the eighteenth century, the Dudley estates lay mainly to the west of the area know as the Black Country, especially in Dudley, Sedgley and Brierley Hill. Dudley Castle had been the family home until the Civil War, when they moved west to Himley Hall. As the Black Country economy started to grow, especially after the introduction of the first Birmingham Canal in 1772, successive Lords of Dudley were perfectly situated to make the very most from this growth.

When John Viscount Dudley and Ward (1724–1788) succeeded to the title and estates in 1774, he at once recognised the potential of the vast quantities of mineral wealth trapped below his turf. The problem lay in the practical difficulties of getting those items to his customers. Set adjacent to the Birmingham plateaux there were no navigable rivers, and only a handful of poor roads.

Straight away he set about improving communications, with the construction of turnpike roads, horse-drawn tramways, and more importantly, taking advantage of and adding to the newly opened Birmingham, Staffordshire & Worcestershire Canals. The following year Lord Dudley was the leading promoter of a canal from Stourton, on the Staffordshire & Worcestershire Canal near Kinver, to the town of Stourbridge, 3¼ miles away.

The line was surveyed by Robert Whitworth who had assisted Brindley until his death. At a meeting in Stourbridge in February 1775, it was decided to add a 4-mile branch from here to Dudley. A bill was submitted to Parliament, but because of great opposition from the Birmingham Canal Co. and competing coal masters, it was withdrawn. Undeterred, Lord Dudley and fellow promoters split the proposal, reapplied, and were successful in 1776.

So two cuts, the first from a place called The Fens, near Pensnet, to connect with the Stourbridge at Wordsley Brook, and the second from a place called Black Delph, Brierley Hill. At the same time, Lord Dudley and Thomas Foley – former owners of Witley Court, sponsored a bill for the Dudley Canal to connect to the Stourbridge at Black Delph.

Also in 1775, Lord Ward (Dudley) commenced building a branch from the Brindley Line at Tipton to his coal pits and limestone workings at Castle Hill (present site of the Black Country Museum). This short waterway came to be known as Lord Ward's Canal. In later years, the Birmingham Canal Co. offered to buy this canal, but reneged on the deal saying that Lord Dudley had been amply compensated by the convenience of using the Dudley Canal and paying favourable tolls. No money ever changed hands.

William Humble Ward 1867–1932 and his mother, Georgina Elizabeth Moncrieffe, 1846–1929.

By 1780, the town of Dudley was close to two canal systems; the Birmingham to the East, and the Dudley & Stourbridge to the west. However, the Dudley and Rowley Hills in between proved an enormous obstacle to any connection of the two. The only reasonable answer was to join the two by means of a tunnel. The tunnel and canal entering Lord Dudley's limestone workings would make an ideal 226yd beginning. John Snape carried out a survey assisted by Samuel Bull in 1785, and then set out the line of the tunnel over the hill. The original estimate was of £18,000. After seven years of graft, many difficulties and one sacked engineer, the tunnel was finally opened in 1792.

The wealth of the Black Country, and that of the Lords of Dudley, was growing steadily. Other canals belonging to Lord Dudley included the 1839 1¼-mile 'Lord Ward's Branch', also known as the Pensnett Canal, which began at a junction with the Dudley at Parkhead and linked to the Pensnett Collieries. Near the Fens Pools was a short stub built to serve the Brockmoor collieries and Round Oak works; this was built earlier in 1784.

When John Dudley died in 1788, halfway through the building of the tunnel, he had no children, and the lands and title passed to a distant nephew, John William Dudley & Ward, who carried on with a lukewarm zeal until he died in 1833, unmarried. Apparently he found decision making extremely difficult, and in his latter years took on a madness by where he spoke to himself in two distinct voices, one bass the other high.

Following his death, everything then passed to another nephew, William Dudley & Ward (1817-1885). These were essentially the finest years for the Dudley family, as indeed they were for the fortunes of the Black Country. In 1833, the Estate was held under the authority of four trustees until the new heir became twenty-one years old. He then inherited the capital from around 200 mines, iron smelting works and chemical factories that produced a yearly income of about £100,000 per year. Witley Court itself had been purchased in 1837 by his trustees for £890,000 – the equivalent of over £30 million today. This made the new Earl of Dudley one of the wealthiest men in Britain – and thus in the world. The red-brick Jacobean house of the Foley's was about to be transformed into an Italianate mansion.

The young Lord moved from Himley into Witley in 1846 and married Selina Constance De Burgh, a great society beauty, in 1851. Sadly she died the same year in childbirth, obviously just as much a danger to the wealthy as to the poor. For the next six years he busied himself with the management of the estates and the aggrandisement of the house and gardens, spending in the process the modern equivalent of another £10 million on the project.

When William died in 1885 his son, William Humble Ward, took up residence when he came of age, and the house became the scene of lavish entertainments for his twenty-first birthday in 1888, and again at his marriage to Rachel Anne Gurney, a banking heiress, in 1891. There were still a few decades of great wealth left for the Dudleys and the Black Country's mining industries. The family held shooting parties for royalty and the aristocracy, but there was a decided downturn in both their fortunes as the First World War approached.

Louis XIV-style ballroom at Witley Court, almost the width of the east wing. The ceiling was high to accommodate the four chandeliers. Destroyed by fire along with much of the rest of the house in 1937.

From 1889 onwards the Dudley wealth steadily declined, and in 1913 the Earl was forced to mortgage the Estate and sell paintings to finance his extravagant lifestyle. After the house was sold in 1920, the urns at the bottom of the main stairs were found to be stuffed with unpaid bills. In June 1920, the Countess Rachel was found drowned after a swimming accident at another of their homes in County Galway, Ireland. The Earl married Gertrude Millar, a star of the London music hall, in 1924, and they moved into the original family seat at Himley. He died in 1932.

AT WITLEY COURT

During the 1890s, Witley had about fifty servants in the house, many under the charge of the butler, while the housekeeper took orders for her housemaids from the Countess.

The splendour of Witley Court, south-west face and fountain.

There was also a head cook and gardener with their staff, plus twenty-five gamekeepers, making a total staff of around 130. To heat the house, a giant coal stack of around 1,500 tons was maintained to fuel five hot-water boilers and the dozens of grates around the house. On a cold day the house could consume as much as 30 tons of coal, all carried from the Dudley mines by boat to Shrawley on the River Severn, then 4 miles by horse and cart; a service conducted by the local farm tenants in lieu of rent. It finally reached the house by a concealed track-way to bring it into the house unobserved.

On 7 August 1888, when William Humble Ward came of age, his birthday celebrations extended over three days. Firstly, the Earl and his mother received congratulations from tenants of the Witley, and later the Holt, Estates. That evening the driveways were illuminated by lamps and fairy lights, two marquees were erected, one being for the guest's coachmen, while 240 people from the upper echelons of society attended the ball. A temporary stable was provided for 100 horses. The next day there were more congratulations from near and far, while nearly 900 cottagers sat down to a free luncheon. At night, the grand fountains were illuminated and the third day climaxed with a firework show.

Meanwhile, back in the pits an entirely different scene was grinding on with regular monotony, as men and women worked as many as twelve hours per shift. Families were being robbed of their hard earned money in the Tommy shops, where prices were on average about 30 per cent higher than in regular shops, a situation that generated the food riots. Boys as young as eight years old worked down the mines, while young women graded the coal above ground by hand and hauled coal tubs in harness.

In 1888, deaths down the mines as a consequence of gas explosions, roof falls and accidents in the shaft were actually going down, due in a large part to legislation that had hit the pits from the middle of the 1800s. During the first half of that century, deaths had averaged 150 per annum; approximately 750 for the first fifty years. No wonder that at least one writer on the Black Country referred to the Lords of Dudley as 'the biggest mass murderers the Black Country has ever known'. It goes without saying that they would decry that statement, and point instead to the many charitable efforts they made such as the later provision of schools and the erection of the odd church or two. Certainly miners themselves and lesser mine managers were prosecuted, but the Earls were seemingly immune from such charges.

Today the ruins of Witley Court, managed by English Heritage, are well worth a visit, demonstrating a world of great extremes built on canals and coal. The house is about 5 miles south-west of Stourport off the A443.

Witley Church, a fine example of baroque, and well worth a visit.

3

BOAT-BUILDING ON THE BIRMINGHAM CANAL NAVIGATIONS

WALTONS BOATYARD

Geoff Walton, now in his seventh decade, came into boat-building with his father, Len, just as the coal trade in the Midlands was drying up and the new vogue for pleasure boating was just taking off. During this important transitional period for the canal system as a whole, father and son used traditional skills that had been employed for constructing boats for 200 years. This is their story.

Dad was a Bilston man, who started his working life on the canal with John Toole's boatyard as an apprentice boat-builder in 1928. He was then fourteen years old, and he came under the tutelage of Arthur Butler. Toole's were engaged in all kinds of canal work, but Arthur and my father focussed totally on the building and repairing of wooden coal boats, of which there were thousands on the BCN alone. Toole's alone operated between 150 and 200 boats. Built in oak and elm, the boats were strong and durable, but the harshness of the coal trade and the changing seasons wrought havoc to the hulls. Some boats were so knocked about, that when they came out of the water, much of the timber had to be stripped away and replaced

Toole's, like many yards, had a sloping slipway to assist in getting boats out of the water. Two heavy sleepers were slid under the hull, and beneath the sleepers went two heavy duty steel tubes to act as rollers. Chains were placed around the boat, and it was then dragged onto the bank by two hand winches. The main merchant supplying timber to boatyards in those days was John S. Hickman's at Monmore Green, Wolverhampton. Sometimes Toole's bought a whole tree, which would be brought to the yard to be sawn in the pit by two men with a long double-handled saw. This work was especially hard for the man in the pit, who was working against gravity; he was known as the underdog.

When I was about eleven, Dad realised that he would do much better if he took the gamble to operate his own business, so he left Toole's to just that. In 1952 he looked around for a suitable site, finding a boatyard at Deepfields, Coseley, on the main Birmingham to Wolverhampton Canal, belonging to J. A. Wright Coal Merchants, and arranged to rent the dock from them. There was space to get four boats out of the water.

From day one he had plenty of work repairing timber coal boats for firms like Hickinbottoms, Stewarts & Lloyds, Holloway's, Ernest Reid at Dudley Port (one of several operators that had the large 'Ampton boats'), Bakers at Highfields, Creswell's of Oldbury, and also J. Toole's, his former employer. These firms were all coal carriers who operated horse-drawn and motor-driven boats. In those days the coal men worked their boats constantly, and money seemed no object if their boat was out of action. There was a never-ending procession of boats travelling the mainline in the 1950s, either going to or from the Cannock and Brownhills pits.

I remember that Dad was out of the house by 6.30a.m., and in the summer months he wouldn't finish work until it was dark. Mother hardly saw him, so from time to time she would catch a bus along to the yard to see how he was getting on and deliver some well-earned sandwiches. To go to Deepfields in those days was like taking a trip into the countryside, for it was surrounded by pleasant woods. Helping him out part time was Arthur Butler, his former teacher. Arthur had, by then, retired, but he loved working with Dad and he would go in for the morning; it was a way of making a few coppers in his retirement. Even though he was in his seventies, he would walk the 5 miles from his home to the yard, and Dad was fortunate to have him because some of the work, such as steaming and bending planks, required two hands. Much of the work was done using hand tools such as chisels and adzes, but Dad did have a power drill and saw when I went to work with him.

J. L. WALTON & SON
(BOATBUILDERS)

BIDDINGS LANE · COSELEY · STAFFS.

PHONE : BILSTON 42725-6

J.L. Walton's business address.

When I started work at Deepfields in 1956 at the age of fifteen, I began with the simple chores like boiling-up the pitch and tar. This sticky black stuff came from the Midland Tar Distillers at Monmore Green. These two products were mixed, hot, in a drum over an open fire, and you were very careful that the boiling sticky liquid didn't drop onto bare flesh, or that it caught fire; both options were pretty disastrous. Before the blacking was applied, the butt joints needed to be caulked or sealed. This was a long hard job, and I recall that one hull would take from one to two weeks to fully caulk. Hemp was rolled into lengths and then driven between the seams, using caulking chisels and mallets. The chisels were frequently dipped into oil to help them slide between the planking. Only then was the tar applied to the boat's hull with a tar mop, very much like an ordinary mop really – you dipped your mop into the hot tar and then spread it over the exposed timbers and caulking.

On other days I would spend hours cutting up plugs. For this, you took a log of wood and then cut it up into small sticks until they were 3-4in. long and about 0.5-0.75in. sq., then sharpened at one end. These plugs were then ready for repairs. As soon as a boat came out of the water, the strips of metal plating around the footings that protected the boat against ice and general knocks and scrapes would need to be completely removed, as would the plating around the bows. Once this was removed you could then assess the condition of the planking beneath. All rotten timbers would be replaced, and the plugs would be driven in to fill any small holes. Chalico – a mixture of horse manure and tar – would fill and seal any remaining cracks. While the chalico was still soft, new plating would be nailed into place. After being at the yard for some months, I progressed on to plating. Metal plate was delivered to the yard in thin sheets and then cut into a variety of widths. Holes would then be punched into the plate ready to take the galvanised nails.

As I improved my woodworking skills, I moved on to sheathing. After the outer planking of the hull was complete, the inner hull was lined with soft wood. Nailed between the knees, the sheathing added tremendous strength to the craft by holding the planks together. The sheathing also gave you something to caulk up to, and it protected the planking from the continual bashing from coal carrying. I then progressed on to cutting, steaming and fitting the outer planks. Coal boats were, by nature, very square in their design, but there were several curved planks around the bow and stern that required special handling.

PLANK STEAMING

Our steamer was powered by a 40 gallon steel drum that lay across an open fire. This was our receptacle for boiling water. Close to the boiler was the steam box, a large timber box made from thick boat planking, and the steam was delivered from boiler to box via a 2in. steel tube. After being cut to size, each plank was placed inside the steam box, and the ends were sealed to keep in the heat while the plank was steamed for between 1.5-2 hours; timing came from experience. A 12ft oak plank with a thickness of 2in. that had gone in as stiff as a proverbial board would then emerge from the box in quite a floppy state. You then had about fifteen minutes to get it clamped into position. The next day it would be nailed into place. It was only possible to work between two and four planks each day.

If we were building a new boat from scratch, we started with the bottom planks first, all resting on trestles. Next came the stem and stern post, after which the keelson, or backbone, of the boat would be laid down and bolted to the base planks. The keelson to our boats used to be bolted with four and a half inch bolts. The bottom strakes were cut to a template and then the vertical knees that acted as ribs, and thus shape, for the boat, were cut and set into the base. Each boat-builder had his own particular ways and preferences; we always used timber knees instead of steel, once these were in place the main planking could then be nailed to them.

Once the cabin was painted, Dad would set himself to the sign writing and the boat would be ready to go off to its new owner. Dad was a man of many skills and talents but he wasn't – to my knowledge – artistic, so he never did paint roses and castles or stuff like that, but he was pretty good at lettering which included the boat's official number. He never attended college, but he did do a home sign-writing course where he would practise setting out and painting letters on a board before sending them away for assessment.

Lettering was set out on the cabin sides using chalk and lines. For this you took a string line and rub chalk along its length. After measuring up the cabin, the line was stretched tight, held against the measured points and twanged into place; this left a nice chalk line against which to set the letters. Once this was done, Dad would tell me to go and get on with something else while he wrote the letters.

CHANGING TIMES

During the 1950s, when I was in my late teens, Dad could see the writing on the wall as far as the coal trade and general canal carrying was concerned. Less and less boats plied the waters, and we were starting to wonder what the future held for repairs and building work. One of my lecturers at Wolverhampton Art School, a Mr Crowley, kept a small pleasure boat, and he brought it along to our yard one day to do some repairs. While he was there, he put the seed of an idea into Dad's mind to build pleasure boats. Thus started a period of great change for us, as indeed it was for the canal system as a whole. It was a kind of sink or swim situation.

So, shortly after, we commenced constructing a 35ft pleasure boat. Dad also bought our very first car, a Morris. As we worked on this innovative project, we talked to friends and family about our new venture, and a Mr Sam Greaves became so interested in the new boat that he bought it before it was complete; this seemed a good omen. Named *Nicola*, it was in some ways similar to a coal boat, but it had a much larger cabin to provide four berths. We fitted the propeller and drive shaft, and Sam installed his own engine.

Above left: Oak knees in place and planking commenced.

Above right: Planking and sheathing completed. Gunwales next to be fitted.

Above left: Jodor, caulked and painted. This four-berth boat was fitted with a Mercedes OM 636 diesel, and went originally to a Jonah Penn of West Bromwich.

Above right: The galley of *Blue Anchor,* how times change.

As soon as *Nicola* had gone, we immediately started work on our second craft, the *Penguin.* By then we were getting a little more adventurous with our designs, and the *Penguin* was more curvaceous in its lines. To this boat we installed a Stewart Turner 4.5hp petrol engine. My woodworking skills had been enhanced by my college training and I fitted out a basic galley to the cabin, complete with Calor gas cooker and chemical toilet, much like in contemporaneous caravans.

We did no advertising, but word quickly got around, and we were soon building a couple of boats for the Aylesbury Boat Company who had gone into the hire trade early. After that, we carried on building for private customers. In the 1960s, John Stothert of Shropshire Union Cruises told us that his company would have every boat that we could build, the deal being that we constructed the hull and superstructure and John would fit out the majority, but not all, of the interiors. The boat would then be ready for resale. So, as the coal trade died off, a new one just as demanding took its place; we were very fortunate.

Above: The *Heart of Oak* at Norbury Junction, 1971.

Left: A newly finished *Jodor.*

4

THE TUB-BOAT CANALS OF SHROPSHIRE

Once upon a time, there were a handful of short canals in the area east of Shrewsbury that is now called Telford. Telford, of course, is a new town. In the late eighteenth century there were much smaller habitations that included Madeley, Dawley, Ketley and Oakengates. Gradually, the region was turning into an industrial heartland.

Operating its own unique 20ft tub boats that carried on average of around 5 tons, this interconnected system kept itself to itself for fifty years or so, until it finally became connected to the main canal network at Norbury Junction in 1835. From that date on it flourished until the early twentieth century when, like so many other canals, its activity ground to a halt. Then, during the second half of that century, much of the routes became obliterated by modern developments or simply reverted back to agriculture.

Now however, with an enormous interest in the revival of inland waterways, the Shrewsbury & Newport Canals Trust is working hard to bring about the reinstatement of at least two of these historic routes. Fortunately, I have been given a handful of photographs from Tom Manning, an ardent supporter of that trust, to illustrate how some of that system appeared during the early 1950s. But how, and why, did those canals appear in the first place?

Inspired by the Duke of Bridgewater's success with his coal canal near Manchester, his brother-in-law, Lord Gower, joined forces with John and Thomas Gilbert in 1764 to construct a 5½-mile canal carrying 3-ton tub boats. The waterway would run from the coal deposits on his Estate at Donnington Wood, past Lilleshall Abbey to Pave Lane on the Wolverhampton road where a wharf would be built. At Donnington Wood, the canal probably connected to other underground navigable mine workings as in the Manchester area. The line to Pave Lane was completed in 1768, and this seems to have been the springboard for other local projects.

Soon after, a branch was built from Hugh's Bridge to limestone quarries near the village of Lilleshall, with a second to Lilleshall lime works, coal wharf and stone pit at Pitchcroft. Coal went in one direction, to burn limestone, and then lime travelled in the opposite direction to the iron furnaces at Donnington. At Hugh's Bridge there was no connection because of a difference in levels of 42ft 8in. At first cranes performed the transhipping procedure, until later when an incline plane (a hill railway) performed the task. We will see how these incline planes came to be extremely popular in this hilly district.

In 1786, Lord Gower was made the Marquis of Stafford, and his son became the Duke of Sutherland. Thus, in 1833, this waterway became known as the Duke of Sutherland's Tub-Boat Canal. Much earlier though, the Coalbrookdale region on the River Severn was turned over to industry and an extensive tram-road system connected associated activities at Horsehay and Ketley. Another leading industrialist, William Reynolds, who ran the Ketley Iron Works, discovered coal and iron at Wombridge. So he built a 1¾-mile canal to connect those workings with the Donnington Wood.

THE SHROPSHIRE CANAL

To build this link to the River Severn, William Reynolds did the initial survey with later assistance from Jessop. Then, with other interested parties, he raised the necessary capital of £50,000. The Shropshire Canal connected with the Donnington via the Wrockwardine plane, 316yds long. This 7¾-mile canal, with a second plane at Windmill Farm, plus three tunnels, ran via Ketley Bank and Madeley to the third Hay incline plane just above the River Severn at Coalport. The ¾-mile Coalport Canal that ran parallel with the River Severn was constructed at the same time, the Hay incline connecting the two. A 2¾-mile branch went to Horsehay and Brierley Hill.

During the same period, William and Richard Reynolds teamed up to build a 1½-mile branch from the Shropshire Canal to Ketley. A plane was built at the Ketley end. The boats that plied this system were 20ft long by 6ft 4in. wide, and they carried 8 tons. Several of them were tied together in trains and towed along by one horse, with guard rails fitted at bends to assist in the turning process.

THE SHREWSBURY CANAL

While the Shropshire Canal was being dug, there was a strong desire for another to take coal into Shrewsbury. That old established town suffered the problems of other sizeable habitations – a poor road system – and thus they paid a high price for bulk goods like coal. Thus, the Shrewsbury Canal Company was formed, of which Reynolds was a director and shareholder. A connection between that canal and the aforementioned system was made at the Trench Incline. A survey was made in 1792 by George Young of Worcester.

Again the promoters were the leading industrialists of Shropshire, who had seen the great advantage of canal building, as well as others who saw the benefits of cheaper coal in Shrewsbury. When complete, it ran a total of 17 miles, from a connection with the Wombridge Canal (in fact a section of the Wombridge was bought for this purpose) to the Trench to Wappenshall branch, before turning west to go to Shrewsbury; though there never was a connection to the River Severn. The practice of using the short tub boats carrying a maximum of 8 tons was again adopted; the traffic, as predicted, was mainly coal to Shrewsbury.

BIRMINGHAM & LIVERPOOL JUNCTION CANAL

In 1825 an ambitious project was born; to take a canal from the Staffordshire & Worcestershire Canal, near Wolverhampton, north to Nantwich. Known initially as the Birmingham & Liverpool Junction Canal, it provided an excellent link from the Midlands through to Chester and Liverpool via the Chester Canal. Engineered by Telford, it opened throughout on 2 March 1835. Meanwhile the operators of the little tub-boat canals immediately saw the benefits of linking their system up with a national scheme. A plan was drawn up in 1827, and a branch to Newport was opened two months before its grander arterial neighbour.

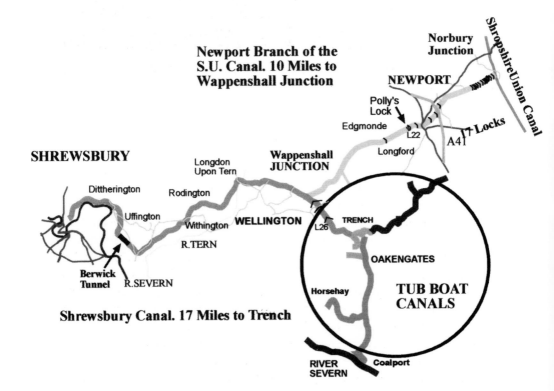

The Shrewsbury Canal and Tub-Boat Canals.

The Hay Incline plane at Coalport. This connected the Shrewsbury Canal to the lower short section of the Coalport.

THE PLANES

Where there were sharp differences in land levels, running a railway up a slope came to be the most favoured solution, except at Coalbrookdale where two 120ft shafts were used and loads were craned up and down. Of course there were the inevitable delays of transhipment, even where the tub boats were transferred directly from the canal and onto the plane.

The Ketley Plane overcame a fall of 73ft, and the tub boats were carried on cradles. The motive power for raising the empties was cleverly performed by gravity, where the downward full tubs raised the empties by a drum and cable system. At the top of the plane was a lock, so that, as the water drained from it, the boat came to rest neatly on the cradle. It was then immediately ready for lowering down the hillside.

The planes on the Shropshire Canal had a slightly different solution. They were designed and built with a reverse slope at the top instead of a lock, and power was provided by a steam engine. The Hay and Windmill Planes were, at first, operated by horses, later being replaced by a combination of counterbalancing and steam power. The plane at Wrockwardine was worked mainly by steam.

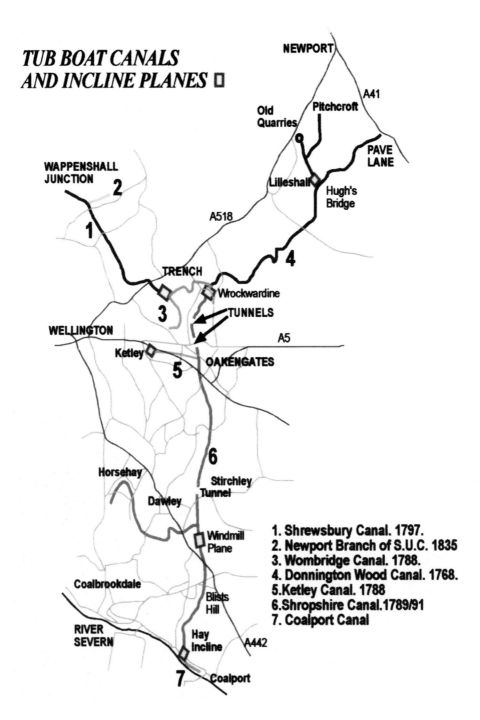

TUB BOAT CANALS AND INCLINE PLANES □

NEWPORT

Old Quarries

Pitchcroft

A41

PAVE LANE

WAPPENSHALL JUNCTION

2

Lilleshall

Hugh's Bridge

A518

1

4

TRENCH

Wrockwardine

3

TUNNELS

WELLINGTON

Ketley

5

A5

OAKENGATES

6

Horsehay

Stirchley Tunnel

Dawley

Windmill Plane

Coalbrookdale

Blists Hill

RIVER SEVERN

Hay Incline

A442

7

Coalport

1. Shrewsbury Canal. 1797.
2. Newport Branch of S.U.C. 1835
3. Wombridge Canal. 1788.
4. Donnington Wood Canal. 1768.
5. Ketley Canal. 1788
6. Shropshire Canal. 1789/91
7. Coalport Canal

The Tub–Boat Canals.

Generally speaking, the planes operated most efficiently, but accidents did happen, and it was most fortunate that one particular incident at the Hay did not result in loss of life or limb. One day, a tub-boat support chain snapped. Immediately, 5 tons of pig iron, plus the weight of the cradle and boat, shot down the hill. So much energy was built up in the fall that, when it reached the bottom, the whole thing bounded into the air, cleared two moored boats and pitched into the river.

CANAL FEATURES

Other interesting features of the tub-boat canals included the Berwick Tunnel on the Shrewsbury line, and the aqueduct at Longdon-Upon-Tern. The 970yd Berwick Tunnel was the first of any length to have a towpath in its design. Baulks of timber were set into one wall, and then timber planking formed the path. Because the towpath projected 3ft over a 10ft waterway, this reduced the resistance of passing boats, similar to that on the Pontcysyllte Aquaduct. The towpath was removed in 1819.

The cast-iron aqueduct at Longdon-Upon-Tern seems to have earned a place in the development and evolution of this material. Apparently though it was not the first, for that honour goes to the one on the Derby Canal, but it does seem to be the second, and an influence toward that ultimate of cast-iron troughs, the Pontcysyllte Aquaduct, mentioned earlier.

The Coalport Canal, right next to the River Severn.

5

TOM MANNING

At this point, I would like to pay a small tribute to a very lovely old gentleman, Tom Manning, who passed away in March 2007 aged ninety-seven. Born in the August of 1910, Tom was ninety-four when I first met him, and his enthusiasm for the canal network – especially the Shrewsbury Canal – was still bright even at that venerable age. He lived in Newport for the last part of his life, and he was as involved as much as he could be, given his age, with the Shrewsbury & Newport Canal Trust. The Trust, as some of you may be aware, has been promoting the reinstatement of the Newport branch of the Shropshire Union Canal to Wappenshall Junction, and the former Shrewsbury Canal that connected the latter to Shrewsbury town.

Section of aquaduct at Longdon-Upon-Tern, c.1950

Norbury Junction on the Shropshire Union, where the Newport Branch starts.

Above left: Lock No.23 on the Newport Branch and Edgmond Wharf, *c.*1950.

Above right: Coal Wharf at the end of the Humber Arm.

He invited me over to his house to give me his collection of photographs that he had been taking of the canals for some sixty years, explaining how he got to be so interested in the waterways. His earliest memories of the canal were from visiting Goldstone Wharf on the Shropshire Union Canal as a child. There he recalled seeing the boats collecting milk churns which were going to Cadbury's at Knighton. Then later, after moving to Newport in 1929, he vividly remembered the coal-carrying boats through what was then a small sleepy village.

As for his photography, he started out with a box camera, before purchasing an Agfa Speedex 120 Folding Record for the sum of £5 shortly after the Second World War. Then, in 1949, he purchased a BSA Bantam 125 motorcycle and started to venture further afield. The beauty of the nearby Welsh canals proved irresistible, but Tom discovered a wealth of English canals too, and was soon planning excursions to the Macclesfield, Peak Forest, Cromford, and as far south as the Kennet & Avon Canal.

Wappenshall Junction. Newport branch is on the left.

Unique picture of one of the original tub boats that plied these canals. Several were tied together to form a train.

A lock on the Humber Arm showing the guillotine gate.

So, it is a pleasure to feature his black and white images of the Shrewsbury & Newport Canals to get a glimpse of what this lovely waterway was like during the 1950s, and to imagine what a wonderful addition to the system it would make – if only it could be restored.

THE FUTURE

As mentioned at the outset, a review of these historical – but generally lost – canals seems appropriate in the light of a recent study undertaken in 2003 to reinstate at least two of these waterways (i.e. the Newport branch and the Shrewsbury Canal). The plan is that the line will stay mainly on its historic route, except for a few small necessary deviations.

At Longdon, the aqueduct, due to its poor condition, would require a steel lining, while a marina with a visitor centre, flanked by café/restaurant would accommodate tourists near Wappenshall. The greatest difference, however, would be at the Shrewsbury end. In the past there was never a link with the river below the town's terminal basin, but the plans now being promoted by the Trust envisage two interesting options, both utilising a lock to make the connection. The prospects are no doubt exciting.

6

FRED BUNN

Throughout my youth, the canals of Cheshire and Staffordshire were my home, playground and workplace. The towns and cities my family regularly visited included Northwich, Manchester, Stoke-on-Trent and, of course, Middlewich, where I still reside. Much of the boating work was either for the 'Potbanks', as they were called in the centre of Stoke-on-Trent, or the extensive salt works around Middlewich. Having said that, a boatman's life was often varied, and my family could have just as easily been heading down the Shroppie to the busy Birmingham canals.

The 1960s was a decade of enormous change. Both of those earlier mentioned industries of pottery manufacture and salt making provided employment not only for their own workers, but for boating companies in and around Cheshire. They both went into decline during the 1960s and were finished by 1970. Before I describe the salt industry, however, which had effectively been running the open pan arrangement for two thousand years, I will relate a bit about my background.

I was born in 1937 to Fred and Elsie Bunn, who at that time worked for Potter & Sons, a sizeable boating company. At first, we lived on a single horse-boat, and as I grew up they taught me all I needed to know about boating craft and looking after horses. Those were the days when children and mothers worked long hours and were paid nothing. Additionally, you had to buy your own horse. A decent horse was between £30–£50 – a lot of money. Later, when at Seddon's, the company would loan you the money to purchase an animal, and then you would pay back half a crown each week. Blacksmiths' work and vet bills were all paid for by the family, not the boating company.

Our cargoes were raw materials, such as china clay and flint for the pottery firms that lined the canal banks at Stoke-on-Trent, and then we boated away the finished crockery to places like Runcorn, Weston Point or right into the heart of Manchester. After years of travelling the Trent & Mersey, Bridgewater and Shropshire Union Canals, you get to know every lock, pound and bridge. Operating locks soon becomes second nature to the child of a boatman. Boats at Potter's included the *Somerset*, with a 125hp Petty, the *Starlight*, which had a 12hp Bollinder, and the *Sunshine* which had the larger 20hp Bollinder.

Skimming salt from the pans. (Cheshire Museums)

Lump men. Blocks of salt have been turned out of their boxes to dry.

Potter and Son's *Sunshine* and *Starlight*.

When I was still a small child, the Second World War started, and Mom and Dad went to work for the much larger firm of Fellows Morton & Clayton. The transfer to a motor-powered boat with a butty was considered a big improvement over horse boating, and our work was centred on the very busy city of Birmingham. To help us cope with the two boats, we were joined by my aunt. During those years, the focus of much boating activity was Crescent Wharf, now long gone. It was a branch canal that came from a junction at the top of the Birmingham 13, and was lined with cranes, boating cargoes and warehouses.

When I was older, Dad told me how one night during the war the Air Raid Precaution warden came to hurry us into the bomb shelters as the Germans were making a raid on the city. It was just as well that we complied with his direction, for a bomb blew away the side of the nearest canal bridge. During those years we carried all kinds of goods, including metals, food and clothing, and tubing from Stewarts & Lloyds at Netherton to the heart of Manchester.

When the war ended we went back to Potter & Sons, where there were still three families operating their boats. They were the Dewhursts, Hollinsheads and the Johnsons. After some time at Potter & Sons, Mom, Dad and I went to work at Seddon's. Seddon's was just one of about a dozen salt-making companies based in Middlewich, and they operated around six of their own horse boats that included the *Badger*, *Stoat* and *Weasel*. They also had *Jean* and *Nora*. Later they had their first motor boat, the *Sweden*. Boats were used to take away the finished salt, much of it to the Anderton lift where it was transferred to the boats down on the River Weaver, or to bring in coal. Much coal was used to fire the salt pans, which I will describe later.

Above: Thurlwood Steel Lock. This used to be on the Trent & Mersey.

Left: Fred Bunn Senior at Weston Point.

Dad went to work with the slack gang. This was a group of three men that emptied out the coal boats by hand, and then transported it in wheel barrows. That was really hard work, and they would empty seven boats each day carrying about 20 tons of coal each. I went to work in the production of salt.

Salt had been made in Middlewich since Roman times, when the naturally occurring brine was heated in lead pans over wood fires. When the Trent & Mersey Canal arrived at the end of the eighteenth century it proved extremely useful to the expansion of the salt trade. At that time, the production of salt developed into the use of specialised buildings with much larger metal pans made of cast-iron plates riveted together. These open pans were able to make a variety of grades of salt by varying the evaporating conditions. Specialist salt was made for both the fishing and the leather-making industries.

The pans – also called ponds – were usually around 20ft wide, 2ft deep and up to 40ft long, (there were longer), and contained brine up to about 1ft in depth. Most Cheshire salt works used supplies of natural or 'wild' brine. This was raised using steam-driven deep-well pumps from timber-lined shafts, dug by hand into the underlying rock salt beds. The ponds were heated by a coal-fired furnace arrangement that poured the heat along horizontal brick flues directly beneath the ponds. Thus, the brine was heated and the excess water driven away so that the salt could be skimmed off and placed into wooden moulds called tubs.

LUMPERS, WALLERS AND LOFTERS

Later, the salt tubs were turned upside down so that the heavy salt blocks could be removed and taken into the hot drying rooms. In those days I worked along with the 'Lumpers', the 'Wallers', and the 'Lofters'. The Lumpers were the men that skimmed off the salt into the wooden tubs, the Wallers – an old salt-making name – made the finer salt, while the Lofters put the salt into the drying rooms. Most of the work we undertook at the salt works was in hot steamy conditions.

To maintain the heating process, the work was organised into a continuous shift pattern, and as many of the workers wore clogs – all made at one shop in the town – there was a great clatter along the streets as the men and women went off to work. Those working in the hot buildings had to drink large volumes of fluid to cope with the water lost through perspiration, but it was no good taking in milk for it curdled in no time!

After the salt lumps were dried hard in the lofts, they were then taken to a large crushing machine which turned them into fine powder. After that the salt was bagged. The usual way of packing salt to keep it dry was to first place it in a fine cotton sack, before placing it into a stronger hessian bag. Women were employed to do most of the salt packing and the sewing up of the bags, and my Mom did that. She would sit there chatting to the other women while sewing away with the long curved needles that they used especially for the job.

Fred Bunn on his boat at Middlewich, 2007.

Fred at Weston Point, 1952.

Of course there was always the problem of keeping salt dry when travelling by narrowboat. So, when we loaded the boats up at the wharf, sacking and straw went in first, and then more straw was used to surround the salt. Special attention was paid to sheeting up the boats in case it rained.

I met and married my wife Phyllis while working at Seddon's, and when the salt industry wound up I spent some years working on the bank before Phyllis and I moved into one of the canal houses at Middlewich. I then had a job working for British Waterways. I was employed on maintenance work which included puddling towpaths, dredging – with the labour-intensive spoon dredger, and a multitude of other necessary maintenance chores.

One of the more unusual jobs that I remember doing was preparing the footings for what became known as the Steel Lock. Apparently, the lock at that point on the Trent &Mersey was continually slipping into the ground, and a massive big lock with a steel framework was planned to solve the problem. It was removed some years ago but I still have a photograph of it.

Sadly, I lost my wife in 2006, but I have some very good friends who love being on the canal network. I have my own boat, usually moored up at Middlewich, and spend as much time as I can cruising the waterways.

7

THOMAS CLAYTON'S CAPTAIN, JOHN BLUNN

When I was born in the quiet pre-war year of 1934, my parents, John Henry and Alice Blunn, were boating for Fellows, Morton & Clayton. They had the motor *Elk* with the butty *Fanny*, and later the *Panther* and *Constance*. They travelled the length and breadth of the country, delivering all kinds of goods, but were based at a depot in Wolverhampton. There was a lot of heavy hauling with Fellows, Morton & Clayton, or simply 'Joshering' as we referred to it, as much of the cargo was loaded and unloaded by hand, 25 tons at a time. We delivered a consignment of uniforms to Castle Fields in Manchester one day. Youngsters like me were rewarded with brass buttons and the like, while Dad was given an overcoat to keep him warm during the long cold hours in the hatches.

While I was a child, Mom and Dad continued with the company until the end of the war, during which time there was a general friendliness between boat crews of all of the different companies. As a consequence, Jack Craddock, who was in charge of the Thomas Clayton fleet at Oldbury, approached my father and asked him if he would be a captain for them. Mom and Dad had developed a good reputation on the boats over the years, and that worked well for them.

Our family had grown considerably through the war years, and on the two boats were mother and father, they slept in the butty's cabin, my five older sisters and one younger sister, who had the motor's cabin, while my brother and I had the side bed on the butty. We never considered those arrangements to be cramped; that was the way it was, and the way it had been, for generations. I think in many ways we viewed ourselves as having a great deal of freedom. A consequence of our itinerant lifestyle was missing out on going to school. Still, we managed to learn to read as the years passed, copying down words that we saw on our travels, or by asking older ones to help us read the occasional comic that we were able to get hold of.

I remember an occasion when we were near Nantwich when my father was extremely distressed over the loss of our horse. Years ago we used to get really thick fogs, and one evening he became separated from the horse at a bridge hole. They searched and searched for the horse for hours, but it was not until the next morning when the fog eventually cleared that they found that the poor thing had fallen in to the canal and drowned. This was a big loss to our family, and it took some time to get over it.

At this point I must mention that parents were constantly anxious in case their offspring should fall in to the canal, and I fell in several times. The first time was when I was only about two years old, and I fell out of the hatches. Someone quickly jumped in to rescue me. On a later occasion we were near Longford Lock, and I was out in front with my sisters, lock wheeling. Fortunately, another boat came around the bend, and it was the captain this time that came to my aid. I was given a cup of salty water to make me vomit, because it was not a good idea to swallow the water in the cut for a variety of reasons.

Claytoning was very different from Joshering; Dad made the change because it brought an end to the heavy manhandling of cargoes. The cargoes were different, the destinations and drops were different, and so were the boats. Whereas the Fellows, Morton & Clayton boats had a typical open hold under cloths, Clayton boats had a decking similar to that of a ship. Planks ran the entire length of the hold, and then shorter curved planks ran across those, forming a very strong structure. The holds were designed to contain liquid cargoes pumped in through hatches on the deck. Inside the hold were partition walls, to prevent a large and heavy liquid cargo from swilling around uncontained. A large number of our pickups were from the many gas works dotted around the Midlands.

John walking the horse, Walsall Canal, 1951.

Mary at Banbury, 1953.

Irwell and *Oka* at Chester, 1950.

Our first boats with Thomas Clayton's were the *Umea* and the *Pinn*. The motor boat was powered by a Bollinder, an engine that injured my father quite badly when one day it backfired and broke his leg. He was on crutches for some time, though fortunately he did receive some compensation. By that time, my older sisters were getting married and going on to boats of their own. Mary married Tom Powell, another Clayton's captain. Sadly their first child died when they were boating near Ellesmere Port. My other sister, Liza, married Joe Theobald who had a Clayton horse-boat, while Helen married Albert Clowes who had the Spey and Ohio.

Suddenly, at the age of only forty-six, my father died as we were going through Audlem on the Shroppie. He had been complaining of feeling unwell and had gone into Audlem to seek out a doctor. After some time, my mother sent me to find out where he was. I was thirteen years old at the time. After walking some distance, I came across a crowd, and pushed my way to the front where I discovered my father on the floor. After the burial, we had to make some alterations.

Tom and Mary operated the *Tay*, while mother, my younger brother Bill and I went on to the butty. My other sisters, Doris and Irene, went with Helen and Albert. This arrangement worked well for several years. Much of our work during these years was on the regular runs from Oldbury to Ellesmere Port. We collected fuel oil from the Stanlow Depot and took it back to Langley, near Oldbury. It took only about thirty minutes to load a boat. We did one journey up and down the Shropshire Union Canal each week.

Albert Clowes at Oldbury with *Oka* in 1950. He married John's sister Helen.

John Blunn with
Cath Turpin on
Stour's deck. Clayton
gathering, 2006.

When I was seventeen I was able to become a captain myself (women were not allowed), and I was given the horse-boat *Irwell* and later the *Erne* (Clayton's boats were all named after rivers). Often we would start out at 3 or 4a.m. and make our way along the canals of the BCN towards Windsor Street Gas Works in Nechells. We would collect a load of tar and take it to the Midland Tar Distillery that was based at the bottom of the Titford Canal, not far from Clayton's base. We regularly boated creosote to Four Ashes on the Staffordshire & Worcestershire Canal. Sometimes, if we finished work early, 'Caggy' Stevens (the last horse-boater on the BCN) would pay me and Joe Chattin a pound to take a full rubbish boat to Moxley near Bilston, and then bring an empty one back. He would say, 'take Old Jim with you' (Old Jim being one of Caggy's horses).

Shortly after that I started to court Mary, who also worked for Thomas Clayton with her granddad, Steve Dulson. Steve had been a horse-boater for many years, but even he had to take on a motor boat when they moved to Samuel Barlow's. This meant that I rarely saw Mary, as their work was generally in the Coventry area. So, in 1954 I left Clayton's and my last boat, the *Dove*.

Barlow's were probably operating twenty pairs of boats during the mid-1950s from Braunston, and I started working there along with Steve. He was captain of the motor *Daphne,* which hauled the *Matilda. Beattie* and *Little Marvel* also worked as a pair. I had the *Little Marvel* for a while until Mary and I got married, and then we worked together on the same pair. Barlow's concentrated on the coal trade, and we loaded up with coal from any one of the Coventry pits and then delivered it down the Grand Union to mills and factories at Apsley, Croxley and Langley. We also delivered coal to the jam factory near Bulls Bridge Junction, now commonly referred to as the 'Jam Ole Run'.

Giffard's deck and hatch, also 2006.

Then, in 1959, we had to make a big change in our life. The long runs finished and even the coal trade seemed to be dying off, and we went to live near Coventry for just over a decade. However, working in a factory made us pine for the freedom of the waterways. So we applied to British Waterways and thankfully were offered the house at Wheaton Aston Lock, a delightful rural location on the Shropshire Union Canal. For the next two decades I helped to pile many miles of towpath along the Staffordshire & Worcestershire and the Shroppie, thus keeping the canals open for the new generation of leisure craft.

Many folk remember 1976 as the year of the hot summer. Well, during that scorching July and August, I worked twelve hours a day at the Wheaton Aston Lock, helping boats through, being friendly to the crews, and making sure that precious water was not wasted. For that I received a golden windlass for outstanding service. Once a boatmen always a boatman, so the saying goes, and now, in my seventies, I still live by the canal at Penkridge and often have the pleasure of working with old friends as we transport the historic boats like Gifford and Stour around the waterways.

8

THOMAS CLAYTON'S
OF OLDBURY 1904–1966

Following that last piece about John Blunn, it seems a fine opportunity to look at the famous liquid-carrying firm that he worked for. On 8 and 9 July 2006, a gathering of working boats was held on the Titford Canal, Oldbury. The date was chosen to especially commemorate the final operations, forty years previously, of the famous Midland narrowboat fleet belonging to Thomas Clayton of Oldbury. This fleet had been one of the most successful and colourful boating organisations on the Midlands canals.

Over its busy lifetime of almost 100 years, the Clayton fleet operated a total of 140 boats, most of which were especially built for its distinctive work. From its first registered boat, the *Dove* in 1879, the fleet grew to a maximum of ninety-four at one time before the last boat to pick up a cargo, the *Stour*, collected a hold full of tar from Walsall Gas Works in March 1966.

In the summer of 2006, there were still one or two men and women alive who could relate the tale of what it was like to work and live on board one of those narrowboats, with their cramped but homely cabins. Now in their seventies and eighties, they include John Blunn, Joe Safe, Enoch and Mary Clowes and Maureen Shaw, a few of whom were able to go along to the pump house.

The *Dove* (in fact there were three *Doves* altogether, because as one became unusable a new boat would take its place) was a horse-drawn boat, and would set the trend for the next seventy-eight years, until the company had their first motor boat, the *Soar*, in 1937. This introduction of Bollinder-powered craft, however, did not instantly bring the horse-drawn era to an end. Clayton's went on to use horses for another two decades, the advantage of using a horse being that there was no loss of carrying weight to an engine and its load of diesel. Also, many captains were fiercely loyal to their horse-drawn way of working and were unwilling to change.

As previously mentioned, the Clayton fleet were not like other boats on the system. Designed to carry liquids, the hold was constructed in two compartments to accommodate the cargoes of tar, creosote, oil and gas water. The complete hold was then covered over with a curved double layer of wooden boards, and looked much like the deck of a ship. Cargoes were pumped in at the start of a journey, generally at one of the many gas works dotted around the Midlands, and pumped out at its final destination.

When William Clayton, father of Thomas Clayton and originator of the company, came to Birmingham in the early 1850s, gas works were being constructed as the new source of light and heat. Coal was heated in a controlled process to produce gas, and during that process the by-products of tar, coke and gas oil were produced. William had been a boatman for some time and saw an opportunity. He quickly made business arrangements to transport away those liquid products, as most gas works were close to a canal. These materials became valuable for road building and the fledgling chemical industries. The fleet rapidly expanded to meet these needs, with fiteen boats in 1889 alone.

When Thomas Clayton took over from his father and moved the business to Oldbury, the company saw its finest period during the first half of the twentieth century. After the Second World War, the company, like all other boat operators, started to lose their business for a variety of reasons. This was especially so for Clayton's when North Sea gas started to come online during the 1960s and 1970s, when the old method of making gas from coal came to an end. Many gas works closed between 1961 and 1968. During the 1950s, however, the shipping of another liquid helped to keep the Clayton fleet busy. The company had a contract with Shell to boat fuel oil from its refinery at Stanlow, near Ellesmere Port, back to Shell's depot at Langley, Oldbury.

During the war years, John Blunn's parents, John and Alice, were working for Fellows, Morton & Clayton, though they were tempted enough to go and boat for Clayton's. The advantages of this move meant that all of the previous heavy trans-shipment of cargoes for John and his wife became a thing of the past. The family immediately moved their few possessions onto a motor boat and butty. This working pair arrangement had come to be common on the narrow canals. It provided more accommodation for a growing family, but importantly it meant that one diesel engine could pull twice the load.

The two small cabins of the boats became home to ten people. Their first two boats were the *Umea* and the *Pinn* (most of Clayton's boats were named after rivers). When John Blunn junior grew up, he also became a captain in the Clayton fleet. One of his five sisters married Joe Theobald, who was still working one of the few remaining horse boats, while a second married Albert Clowes, and they had the *Spey* and *Ohio*.

A trip from Oldbury and up the Shropshire Union Canal to Ellesmere Port and back took exactly a week. The Langley Shell Depot was just a short way up the Titford Canal, less than a mile from Clayton's base near Oldbury Junction on the Old Main Line of 1772.

During the 1940s and 1950s, Harry Clayton was managing director (Thomas had died in 1927), with Mr Craddock as manager at the Oldbury Yard. The busy depot mooring was often occupied by dozens of boats as they called for their orders. The yard was equipped with its own blacksmiths, stables, stores and offices. There was plenty of space to take boats out of the water for repairs, and a large metal roof could be moved on rollers to cover the boat and its workmen. Dicky Gibbs worked in the yard, while Fred Winnett did the decorative paint work. A large barrel filled with concrete was conveniently kept to place on the gunwales of a boat. This made the boat tip so that all of the cargo could be pumped out.

Early 1960s. Bill Beech with the *Tay* and a second Clayton boat bringing tar from the Swan Village (West Bromwich) Gas Works back to the Midland Tar Distillery at Oldbury. (D. Wilson)

Rear of *Stour* and *Gifford* demonstrating their cabins. *Gifford* was built in 1926 at Braunston as a horse-drawn craft until the 1940s when it became a butty to a motor boat. After finishing work in 1963, it became one of the first boats in the Boat Museum's (Ellesmere Port) collection in 1976. It was restored by Malcolm Webster at Malkins Bank on the Trent & Mersey Canal in the 1990s.

Left: The Bollinder engine fitted in the engine room of *Stour.*

Below: The *Stour and Gifford* showing the decking and hatch arrangements.

Left: The *Kama* and the *Oka* at Leamington in the early 1950s with boat operator Steve Dulson and his granddaughters Mary and June.

Below: The *'Severn'* coming up the Wolverhampton 21, 1962. (D. Wilson)

Of course, not all boats were employed on the Stanlow run. Others went off to gas works near and far, many in the Black Country, but some as far away as Leamington, Oxford and Banbury. Boat loads of creosote were taken the relatively short distance from Majors Tar Works at Monmore Green, Wolverhampton, over to Four Ashes on the Staffordshire & Worcestershire Canal. Much of the gas water from the gas works went to Robinsons Chemicals at Ryder's Green Junction, near Great Bridge.

Spey and *Ohio* in the 1950s coming back along the Shropshire Union Canal with Irene and Helen Blunn.

Tom Powell on the *Spey* early 1960s, cutting a way through the ice on the Old Wednesbury Canal toward Pudding Green Junction. (D. Wilson)

The *Tay* at Pudding Green (West Bromwich). The original Clayton's colourful sign-writing scheme was followed by this simple but unattractive design for a time after the Second World War.

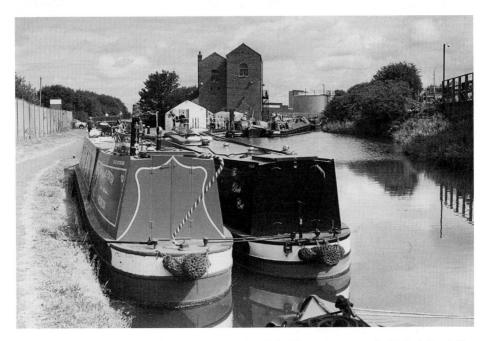

The working boat gathering of 8/9 July 2006, at the Titford Pump house on the Titford Canal. The meeting had special emphasis on the commemoration of the fortieth year since the Thomas Clayton Fleet stopped operating in the summer of 1966.

Working for Clayton's during the middle of the twentieth century was very much a family affair, though family members did not always work the same boats. About this time, the Smiths had the *Severn* and *Gifford*; Annie Tolley and her sons were on the *Usk*; George Clowes and family with the *Ribble*; Tom Powell with the *Tay*; Enoch Clowes on the *Dane*; the Beeches with the *Stour* and *Gipping*; and Charlie Roberts and family on the *Towy* and *Orwell*.

Bill Beech with the *Spey* and *Ohio*, heading for Pudding Green. (D. Wilson)

When the children grew up, they often married members of other Clayton families and carried on the boating tradition. Enoch and Mary Clowes were of this number. After getting married in 1944 they were given the *Hebble*. The wooden, horse-drawn *Hebble* had been introduced to the fleet back in December of 1927, and was built by Rudkin Brothers of Leicester.

At the end of the war, Enoch was paid £4 10s for the five-day run up to Stanlow and back. The Clowes left Clayton's, along with other families who had boated for the company for two or more generations, as the work started to dry up.

Thomas Clayton's were one of the last big companies to work on the BCN. Out of the 140 boats, twenty-one survive, many as converted recreational craft like the *Dove, Adder* and *Captain*. Others, such as the *Stour* (motor boat) and *Gifford* (horse boat), have been lovingly and carefully restored into superb condition in order to keep that important and fascinating part of our industrial heritage alive in the twenty-first century.

For more information on the history of this company, see Claytons of Oldbury *by Alan H. Faulkner, or* Narrowboat *issue spring 2006.*

9

ARTHUR DUFFIELD

My how things have changed since the 1930s and 1940s when I was a young man. The old Black Country town of Tipton has altered almost beyond recognition. In those days the main thoroughfare of Owen Street was fronted by dark Victorian shops, with separate butchers, bakers and clothes shops. The nearest thing to a supermarket was the Cooperative that appeared just before the war, and that was nothing like the supermarkets of today.

My father was John Duffield and we lived right by the junction of the Old Birmingham Canal, engineered by Brindley, and the Tipton Green Locks Branch. This was the start of what was then the Tipton Green & Toll End Communication Canal that ran east to join the Walsall Canal. At the junction was Whittaker's Coal Wharf and across the canal was Tipton Flour Mill, which received its grain by boat. Mitchard's Coal Wharf was just under Owen Street Bridge opposite the Fountain Inn.

Perhaps the most unusual crew to deliver to this mill during the Second World War were the three females that included Eily Gayford, who wrote the book *The Amateur Boatwomen*. In that book she described her experience of a delivery from Worcester to Tipton on the narrowboat *Heather Bell* in 1941:

> The next morning unloading started soon after ten. The method was rather simple: a chain was lowered into the boat, and when it had been fixed round the neck of a grain bag, men pulled on it, up went the bag and down came the other end of the chain ready for the next.

Along with my three brothers and two sisters, we lived in a house that had formerly been the White Horse pub. Before I was born, my father had boated for Hickman & Pitts Coal Merchants near Dudley Road Bridge, but when I was a youngster he was working for William Elwell & Sons of Tipton, a large and well-known coal merchants.

Elwells Coal Yard was sandwiched between the canal and Malthouse Row, just along the canal from the Malt House Stables which were refurbished a few years back to serve Sandwell Council for leisure activities. My Uncle Ted also worked there. Elwell's operated eight or nine boats (this number included three of the large Hampton boats), with a similar number of horses, and had a length of wharfage for about four boats to dock end to end.

Arthur Duffield, 2004.

My uncle Hector also worked on the waterways with his own spoon dredger, which he operated around the BCN with two other men. They bow hauled it from one place to another, empty or full. Hector generally got his orders from Dan Mills, another coal merchants situated at the end of the Haines Branch in Great Bridge.

In those days there was never much clearance between the bottom of the boat and the bottom of the cut, and when arms and basins regularly silted up and boat movements were hampered, factory owners were quick to call in the spoon dredger in order that their livelihood would not be hindered. Dredging was a never-ending and vital way of keeping the waterways open for business. Hector Lived in Horseshoe Row, right next to the first lock, as did the Cartwrights. Some of the Cartwright family were boaters, while a few of them were famous locally as boxers.

A Black Country postcard showing the canal as it winds past the Malt House Stables during the 1930s. Elwell's coal yard is in the distance.

Coal being unloaded out of 'Ampton' Boats, one being the *Iris May* at Mitchard's Wharf, Tipton. The lorries were operated by Potts.

Map of Tipton Green showing the old 1772 line, and new 1830s line.

Of course the most famous boxer for us was the Tipton Slasher, the bare-knuckle champion of England, who in the second half of the nineteenth century owned the Fountain Inn on the opposite side of the junction from where we lived. Men who worked hard argued that going to the pub was one of the few pleasures in life; certainly pubs were an important part of social life in the first half of the twentieth century and were liberally sprinkled throughout the town. Sited at the junction was the Beehive public house, and at the end of the pub stood a unique toll office made of cast iron; it was removed just before the war.

After elementary education at Tipton Green and then Park Lane School, I left education in 1936 at the age of fourteen and immediately went to work with Dad. Normal school hours were now a thing of the past, for we arrived at Elwell's yard at midnight on Sunday, ready to get our horse-drawn coal boat over to the mines early the next morning. Our destination was The Grove Pit, some 14 miles away on the Cannock Extension Canal.

So, with only the moon for light, I untied the boat and pushed it away from the wharf towards the opposite bank and jumped on board, while Dad walked the horse over Owen Street Bridge toward the Fountain Inn. We swapped jobs at Horseley Fields Junction; I drove the horse while dad took over on the tiller. This was to be our routine for several years to come. The Grove was the first pit on the left after turning left at Pelsall Junction onto the Cannock Canal. It was light when we arrived.

The coal mines, with their horizontal subterranean passageways, riddled the ground around Cannock and Brownhills, and that had a direct effect on what went on at the surface. Sometimes you could sit and watch the land sink down with your own eyes. On one occasion, a tug was taking four empty boats under Badgers Bridge when the bridge and surrounding land started to sink. The first three boats made it but not the last one.

Barkers Coal Wharf, Tipton. Factory Locks. (K. Hodgkins)

At the side of the Fair Lady Colliery was a clay pit from where the canal company obtained fresh clay for building up and doing repairs to the cut, caused in most instances by subsidence. When you arrived at one of the pits, you either tied up the boat you were on and took away a full one, or you waited to have your empty one loaded.

Each pit had its own arrangements for getting the boats loaded up. At the Grove Pit, coal came rattling down chutes, while at Leacroft, small pit ponies pulled trucks that we called dobbins along a railway to the boats. Ponies that for some years had only known the gloomy environment of the underground workings were, in their later years, given the privilege of hauling trucks up in the sunlight; it was hard for both men and animals.

Tempted by a boatman named Scotty who worked for the Oldbury firm of T.S. Elements, I went with him boating coal from Hednesford to the power station at Stourport on what we referred to as 'The Light Run'. In those days you used to be able to come out of the Cannock Extension Canal and then turn west, to pass through the Churchbridge Locks, before joining the Staffordshire & Worcestershire at Hatherton Junction. That section of the BCN disappeared long ago. Elements ran a rota for the boats which changed from week to week, with many of the runs commencing just after midnight. After a month of that punishing routine I had had enough, and returned to Elwells.

When the war came along in 1939, I and many other young men were prevented from joining the armed forces due to the fact that canal transport was classed as a vital contribution to the national war effort. We were all classed as 'Bevin Boys', as were all the other men working down the nation's pits. Work for us carried on much as normal, except for in the evenings when stop planks were positioned at regular intervals to divide the canal off into sections. This was in case a bomb caused a breach. We were pleased about this because at least it regulated the hours that we could work.

During the war, Elwells purchased two motor boats, the *Tiptonian* and the *Progress*. I believe that the *Tiptonian* eventually went to Caggy Stevens, while the Petter-powered *Progress* went to Leonard Leigh, another big coal carrier. The company also started using two small lorries, Ford one-tonners. I obtained my provisional licence in 1939, the year the war broke out, which meant that I could either work the boats or go out delivering. In the yard the coal was weighed, put into rough brown sacks and then placed onto a truck. Then I would go off to deliver to private homes all over the Black Country. Most households had a delivery every two to four weeks.

When carrying the coal to the house, I wore a large leather shoulder pad; this gave some protection from the weight and from the large sharp lumps in the sack. The horses did not get such pampered treatment; after hauling the coal boat for many hours, the leather collar they wore often rubbed their necks raw, and the only treatment was salt water to harden off the skin. They were not too pleased with that, as you can well imagine.

In those days every one used coal, either in the black leaded kitchen range or on an open fire, and most houses had a coal shed or bunker to keep it in. Indoors, next to the hearth, were kept the ubiquitous fire irons. The set generally comprised a poker, coal tongues, shovel and brush. Nowadays these items are sometimes used as ornaments, and the younger generation wonder what on earth they were for.

Compared to other companies, Elwells looked after their horses, and they employed a horse fettler to prepare their food. He had a kind of hand-operated machine for cutting up the hay. Tommy Brindle was the nearest farrier, and he had a place at the other end of Owen Street near the railway station. Often the horses would do so much walking that they wore their shoes out in as little as three weeks, so I would take two or three at a time to have new shoes fitted. Usually, Tommy would say 'Come back in a couple of hours,' but occasionally I would stay and watch him make the shoes.

In and out of the fire went the iron, and when it was glowing bright red, Tommy would hammer it around the curved horn of the anvil until it was the correct size. Of course, every now and then the bosses would take a trip out with the fettler and come back with a new horse; this was the prelude for fun and games as we got the newcomer trained up. During the first few days you would always have one man to lead with a bridle, while the other man was behind on the reins.

After the war, Elwells started to move away from canal transport and into the scrap metal business, becoming Elwell & Brown. Shortly after this, my brother and I went to work for the BCN Company at their Sneyd Depot a couple of miles north of Walsall. Billy Holt was the gaffer at Sneyd, while the district foreman at the larger depot at Ocker Hill was Jack Aston. My brother Jack went labouring with a gang on canal repairs; I went to work on one of the two spoon dredgers that were based at Sneyd. Those were the days before widespread automation and the use of hydraulics for digging, and the workings of a spoon dredger were very different.

The boat was pretty much a normal open boat, but fitted to it was a large metal scoop, about 4ft long, connected to the end of a wooden arm. This was the contraption which was used to dig the silt and muck from the bottom of the canal. This 'spoon', drilled with holes to allow the water to escape, was lowered and dragged along the bottom of the canal by a winch. The spoon dredger required three men to operate it and I went first on to the winch, but we all swapped around at regular intervals. The work was very hard and we definitely earned our 4s 7d per ton.

The other members of the crew were Harry Forester and Norman Atkins. If we were digging up silt, we would drag 22-23 tons of the stuff into the hold in two or three hours. If the bottom was hard, then the time to fill the boat would be considerably longer. Once full, we would then bow haul the boat to the nearest dump and then shovel the stuff for a second time using shovels, mud barrows and planks to get from boat to shore. On the odd occasion that we loaded up with waste that would burn, we would make our way over to Ocker Hill. At that depot were massive steam engines powered by Lancaster boilers and the waste went into one of them.

During winter months, many of the men would be press ganged onto one of the ice boats, one of which was kept at the Sneyd Depot. The winter of 1947 was the worst freeze I ever witnessed. Our gang used the ice breaker *Laplander* that was kept at James Bridge, near Moxley. At 6a.m. we made our way to the bottom lock on Walsall Canal and cleared the short Town Arm, turned round and came back to the Tame Valley Junction where we set off for the Perry Bar Locks, turned round again and came back to Moxley. If we were lucky we might finish at 8a.m.

Throughout the day we kept a fire bucket burning away at the fore end of the boat. When we occasionally stopped for a quick break, someone would boil up some water over the fire bucket and make tea. That was our only comfort for the day. When the ice boat went down the Tame Valley Canal toward Rushall Junction, we had the advantage of two towpaths, because it was a late canal. So we pulled the boat with seven horses on each towpath, and took eight horses along as spares. The ice boats continued to clear the way until the ice became so thick that even this activity was curtailed. In 1947, the company's experts went and drilled holes in a basin to test the thickness of the ice. The report came back that there was very little water that had not turned to ice. That was one hell of a winter.

One year later the canal system was totally transformed. Out went the old BCN, and in came the British Transport Commission and British Waterways in 1948. I worked the spoon dredger until 1952, when I decided to go to Bradley & Foster's Iron Foundry; but I had not quite finished with the canal. Not living far from Toole's yard at Coseley, I would often see Harold Nightingale, who would say to me, 'Want to earn a few extra bob?' And I would go down to the yard to shovel coal out of the big Ampton boats, either *Jeremy* or *Jill* that carried 50 tons each. Ah those were the days.

10

MEMORIES OF OCKER HILL
BCN DEPOT

I wrote about the Ocker Hill depot in my first book, *Boats, Smoke, Steam and Folk*, discussing the operations going at that important BCN location. However, knowledge is always incomplete and in more recent years I have been able to contact two very amiable gentleman who actually lived there as young men during the Second World War. These are their experiences and pictures.

When the BCN Ocker Hill Depot closed in 1960, it really marked the end of an era. Before that date, carpenters still used tar and horse manure for glue, and adzes to trim timber, steam engines drove all machinery, horses pulled coal boats and many families fattened up a pig or two at the end of the garden. But what was the depot's origin? How did it come to be the centre for most of the operations on the old BCN? And are there any memories of its existence?

Ocker Hill is an unusual name, and there seems to be two possibilities for its origin. One is that a farmer named Okell lived here at some time; however, the most likely explanation comes from Plots map, which describes the place in 1686 as Ochre Hill. The area has large clay deposits, but in the immediate vicinity of the hill were layers of orange ochre soils that easily stain the hands. This ochre was probably used in pottery manufacture. There were also substantial coal measures, and pits were already being dug when Brindley came to route the canal.

So it is not surprising that when the Act was obtained in February 1768, it included a 5–8-mile branch to Ocker Hill. A wharf was conveniently constructed almost next to the turnpike road that ran to Wednesbury. Its use as a pumping station was, however, still in the future. Close by were three lime kilns and a short basin was built so that limestone and coal could be boated in to make burnt lime ready for sale.

The Ocker Hill Branch connected to the Wolverhampton Level of 473ft, a level that locked down considerably to its initial junction with the Staffordshire & Worcestershire Canal at Aldersley. As time went by, and the canal system grew by leaps and bounds, this high canal began to lose water down a variety of locks in a number of different directions, and water supply came to be the big issue. Ultimately the network came to total 159 miles of canal with no fewer that 550 private basins. To cope with this high demand for water, four special reservoirs were built and the company started negotiations with the firm of Boulton & Watt to purchase steam engines for the purpose of back pumping water.

When the Broadwaters Canal (later the Walsall Canal) and Ryder's Green Locks were being planned, the company's engineers realised that, though the two canals were going to be separated by a fall of 65ft, they would pass each other at Ocker Hill by only a few hundred yards. So, plans were drawn up to construct a brick tunnel from the Walsall Canal, through the hillside, and terminate 65ft underneath the wharf. Here they would erect a pumping station and equip it with James Watt's latest technology.

The first Boulton & Watt engine was fitted at Ocker Hill in 1784, followed by a second in 1791, a third in 1803, a fourth in 1825, another in 1837 and a further Boulton & Watt engine in 1851. A double-acting beam type by G.&J. Davis was fitted in 1857, a second-hand Cornish device in 1866, and one from the Coalbrookdale Company in 1884. In 1897, the original 1779 Bolton & Watt engine fitted at Smethwick was transferred to Ocker Hill and housed in its own building to preserve it.

When E. A. Pratt came to survey the BCN at the start of the twentieth century, he noted that there were thirteen pumping stations dotted around the system, operating twenty-two engines between them. His account states that Ocker Hill had the most at that date, with four, but the journal of the Railway and Canal Historical Society lists six engines that were at Ocker Hill in 1902. This included two from the Coalbrookdale Co., one from Gilpin and Co. of Pelsall (1866), two Boulton & Watt engines (1837 and 1851), and a double-acting beam engine by G.&J. Davis, purchased second-hand in 1857. All were pumping just over twenty-six million gallons every twenty-four hours (1,062 locks). All BCN engines together were moving 4,080 locks of water every day according to Pratt.

By the early twentieth century, beam engines had had their day, and more efficient, high pressure steam engines had been developed. So, in 1903/4, all of the old-style engines were replaced by three Hathorn Davey Triple Expansion steam engines. The outlay for pumping work alone was around £11,000 per year. However, this was only part of the work at Ocker Hill.

Geoff Kenyon and Brian Ghent were only boys during the Second World War, but their fathers both worked at the yard; these are their memories.

GEOFF KENYON

In 1936, my father, Wilf Kenyon, cycled all the way to Tipton from Derby looking for work. He was fortunate enough to be offered a job as a blacksmith's striker, along with a house within the grounds. The house was in a very bad state but it was, at least, somewhere to live. For hundreds of years, the two-man team of smith and striker had operated as a harmonious pair; the blacksmith generally received the glory as the craftsman, and the striker was viewed as simply a labourer, though actually a good striker was invaluable.

Looking along the Ocker Hill Branch toward the BCN Depot, *c.* 1950.

The pumping house with its triple expansion Hathorn Davey engines. Fitted in 1904. (K. Hodgkins)

During weekends or after work, when there was no one around, I used to play on the boats in the basin. BCN boats were continually coming in for repair, and were often taken out of the water. Timber boats received new planking and had their seams tarred and caulked, while iron boats had fresh panels riveted in place. Lock gates were built by Bill Homer and Harold Abbots. Huge baulks of timber were laid out on the floor ready for marking out and cutting.

When the war came it brought some hardships. My mother and father were Jehovah's Witnesses and were, as a consequence, conscientious objectors. As they would not support the war effort, some people would not speak to them, and one or two shopkeepers refused to serve them.

BRIAN GHENT

My father moved us from Great Wyrley to Tipton in September 1939, just as the war was starting. The company offered us a house in the depot complex. He (Jack) had been a coal miner for some years, but decided to improve his conditions and take the job at the depot as caretaker and boiler stoker. He joined two other full-time stokers, George Clews and Charlie Mason, to keep the boilers – and thus the steam – up twenty-four hours a day. The shifts were 6a.m.–2p.m.; 2p.m.–10p.m., and 10p.m.–6a.m.

Brenda and Janice Ghent, with a view of the basin and footbridge. Behind is the building that housed the James Watt Engine.

Above left: Brian Ghent aged sixteen in 1952, sitting in one of the depot's horse-drawn ice boats – possibly *Shackleton*. Behind is a spoon dredger; these were made and repaired at the yard, amongst many other items.

Above right: Canal arm with moored boats. Mr Ghent with lock gates waiting to be taken on location. Behind is the boat-building workshop.

Jack and Hilda Ghent by the draw bridge, with the long-gone Ocker Hill cooling towers in the distance.

The three Lancashire-style boilers drove the three Hathorn Davey pumping engines, while pressurised steam was piped to other buildings to power all the machinery for the carpenters and engineers. However, Dad's activities were not confined to just this yard, for he often visited other pumping stations around the BCN to check on their engines. On other days, he spent time at Tipton Gauging Station, where every boat went to be initially gauged. Horse-drawn coal boats arrived regularly at the yard, with about 22 tons of slack on board, all of which was emptied by hand. During winter months, a stock pile was kept at one end of the yard to ensure uninterrupted power. Dad was paid 22s 6d for emptying a boat.

Not soon after the war commenced, German aircraft started to make raids into the Midlands, attacking factories and installations vital to the war effort. As a result of this night-time activity, air-raid lookouts were set up on high spots throughout the Birmingham area; we had one right in the yard, which was pretty exciting for us kids, especially as we got to play in it.

The men erected a tall timber watchtower, surrounded and topped by sand bags. Wooden panels that could be lowered on ropes provided the lookout places. Then, every night, two of the men would station themselves in the tower with binoculars and watch the skies. The doctor's surgery in Toll End took a direct hit one night and the doctor was killed. Big guns stationed on the Rowley Hills, opposite, used to blast out at the raiders with little if any success.

Some years into the war, Italian prisoners of war started to make an appearance on the canals. They were employed in dredging and general labouring work on the towpaths. They used to make lovely woven baskets and my mother used hers for years after. Later on, a dozen or more German prisoners used to come to the yard. They were, for the most part, captured Luftwaffe pilots or air crew, and were billeted in a camp some miles away, but occasionally they slept at the depot for two or three nights.

They also did all kinds of labouring jobs, like emptying the slack boats out. There was one big blonde pilot who was very proud of his physique and strength. He used to put me on his shoulders and then push a heavy barrow of slack right to the top of the pile. When he left, he gave me his silk white scarf, and I still have it to this day.

When the war ended, Dad was back to emptying the coal on his own, and one day he discovered a pair of false teeth amidst the slack. In those days false teeth were very expensive, never mind the fact that their owner must have been missing them. So Dad washed them and put the word about that he had them at the yard. Sure enough, about a month later a boatman from Walsall called to collect them. Dad asked him to put them in, just to make sure that they were his before he took off with them.

One bad winter, Dad rescued an injured swan from the ice. He put a splint on its wing and kept it warm near the steam pipes. Soon the swan was following him everywhere, even down to the pub, though the landlord was not too keen. In the spring, the swan returned to the wild, but about eighteen months later she came back to the yard with four of her signets, just to show them off. I had never seen my dad so emotional.

Above: Brenda and Janice in horse boat *Dora* awaiting repair.

Left: Many households kept a pig in those days to supplement their larder; this is Dickie's.

Blacksmiths shop with Dickie Cope on the left and his striker Bill Martin. The bellows for the fire is just behind Dickie.

As for me, the yard was a never-ending source of interest, and I got to know all the men who worked there. Some days I would sit and watch them. Ted Davies was a master blacksmith, and it was an education to see him make chain. The other blacksmith was Dickie Cope; he was Dad's best mate. Bill Aston was a first class carpenter and boat-builder, and when I was a kid he taught me how to use a hammer and nails. For amusement he played the piano and violin, but for a party piece he used to take his bow and one of the carpenter's saws and play that.

Lock gates were made by Bill Homer and Harold Abbots. Huge baulks of timber came to the yard on railway carts drawn by shire horses. Sam Taylor was another carpenter who made the company's door and window frames, barrow wheels and even coffins. He made my sister a pencil case when she passed her exams for Dudley Girls High School.

Close to the yacht house, where the company kept a boat for the managers to go out and examine the canals, was the James Watt engine house. In that building was the world's oldest surviving example of a primitive steam beam engine. On special occasions it was steamed for visitors, and probably one of the most distinguished visitors was the famous Henry Ford. He came over from the United States long before the war, in 1928. Ford was very keen to purchase the Watt engine and take it back to America. He offered the BCN a blank cheque, but fortunately they had no intention of selling that piece of industrial history.

After almost 200 years of operating as a wharf and repair depot, and following a decade of nationalisation, the depot closed its gates for the last time in 1959.

11

WILLIAM PERRY, THE 'TIPTON SLASHER'

Much of what we know about William Perry, also known as the Tipton Slasher, comes from Tom Langley's book published by the Black Country Society around 1970. Recent research, however, has revealed many more details about this extremely interesting product of the mid-nineteenth century. Details of his life, including his rather unusual marriage in 1851 to Ann Maria Challingsworth of Dudley, his alternative occupation as an engine fitter, and his short spell in the workhouse, are just a few of those finds.

From Langley's book, we discover the young William Perry working on the Birmingham canals during the 1830s on the narrowboats. This is a reasonable, and probably true, account, as living only yards from the busy canal network there is no surprise at this. However, we also know now that, as a boy (he started work at seven), he was trained in the skills of rope manufacture. Did he do both? Well, why not? Many of us move from one job to the next.

Ropes today are usually made from the synthetic materials of nylon, polyester or polypropylene, and always by machine, but historically they were made from natural materials by hand, though rope-making devices did become more complicated as time progressed. It was into this world that William Perry went as a youth. The training obviously stayed with him, for he returned to the craft in the busy Tyneside district when in his late forties.

Hemp was the primary material for rope in the past. The hemp plant, a cultivated crop, in most cases grows from 10-15ft (3-4.5m), and it is the support fibres directly under the skin of the plant that prove so useful for making rope. The technical name is bast fibre. The crop is cut, soaked in water to remove the pithy core, and then the plant is beaten to separate the fibre from the stalk. The coarse texture of hemp creates a strong product and allows for a good grip.

Rope manufacture has been an important occupation for thousands of years, for varieties of rope and twine are essential for many other industries. Shipping has traditionally utilised many miles of rope, and rope manufacture was well established in many coastal towns. The growing inland industries of the eighteenth and nineteenth centuries, such as mining and the canal-carrying trade for instance, also required rope and twine. This meant that most large towns and cities had their own rope works. So how would Perry and men of his time have made their rope?

Twisted ropes are made in stages. First, fibres are gathered and spun to form yarns. In early history, spinning was done on a spindle whorl – a weighted stick which was rotated by rolling along the thigh. Later came the spinning wheel, with its foot treadle, but yarns were also spun in walks, from fibre wrapped around a man's waist. A number of these yarns are then twisted together to form strands; strands are then twisted to form a rope.

The twist of the yarn is opposite to that of the strand, which in turn is opposite to that of the rope. This counter-twisting gives strength to the rope. The principle of the walk is that the yarns are stretched out between revolving hooks, up to 300yds apart, and the hooks twist the yarns together. To stop the yarns dropping onto the floor they are supported by horizontal bars, called skirders, every few yards.

When first employed at the rope works, Perry may have started out like all young lads by turning the hooks, assisting the more experienced rope-maker, or learning to coil the ropes ready for sale. Twisted ropes have a preferred direction for coiling. Right-laid rope would have been coiled clockwise to prevent kinking. Cotton lines were much-used for horse-drawn narrowboats in the Midlands, where the horse was usually around 70-80ft from the front of the boat. Due to the constant dropping into the water, picking up grit and then rubbing around bridges under great strain, a typical line would last about six to eight weeks before it was discarded. We will return to Perry's rope-making trade later, when he moves to the north of England.

As has been well reported, Perry went on to learn his fighting arts on the towpath of the Birmingham canals. He then started fighting for money, taking on opponents of increasing notoriety, beating them all, increasing his winnings, and gaining a tremendous reputation at the same time. During the early 1840s, the Slasher was much in London and was promoted and managed by Johnny Broome, who Langley describes as an indifferent pugilist.

Broome kept a sporting public house called The Rising Sun in Air Street, Piccadilly. Two of the most famous fighters of this period were Ben Caunt and the American, Charles Freeman, who happened to be a 7ft giant. Ben Caunt was born in 1815 in Nottinghamshire and was similar in build to Perry. He won several fights but in the end he would not fight the Slasher. In 1842 he returned from America with Freeman and Johnny Broome arranged a match. Articles of agreement were signed on 29 September 1842 at the Castle Tavern, Holborn, between Charles Freeman and William Perry of Tipton. This was to be a fair stand up fight in a 24ft roped ring, half minute time according to the new rules for £100 per side on Tuesday 6 December.

This, then, was the date of the first encounter between Perry and Freeman. When one considers the size and weight difference between the pair – Perry weighed in at 14st while Freeman was a massive 19st 10lb – one can only admire the pluck of Perry. Nevertheless, after fighting seventy rounds in one hour twenty-four minutes, the result was undecided. Darkness had set in, with a fog to make things worse, so that a rematch was organised for later in the month.

The pair fought again on 20 December, and after 39 rounds the Slasher was disqualified for making illegal falls, while Freeman was declared the winner. This was a most unsatisfactory end to the contest. Perry was fresh and eager to continue, while Broome was so mortified he offered to arrange a contest between Perry and Ben Caunt there and then. Caunt replied that he would fight the Slasher, or any man, for £100–£500, and that the money was always ready, but would he? A small tale told by Perry in his later years certainly questions Caunt's resolve.

Perry, along with a couple of his backers, took his stake of £500 to The Champions at The Coach & Horses, St Martins Lane, to confront Ben. While they were deriding him, in walked the Marquis of Waterford and Lord George Bentinck. Lord Henry Beresford, formerly the 3rd Marquis of Waterford and then later Earl of Tyrone, was frequently in the news during the 1830s for drunken brawling, brutal jokes and vandalism. Reputedly, in 1837, when celebrating a successful fox hunt, Lord Waterford and his party found several tins of red paint which they daubed liberally on the buildings of the High Street of Melton Mowbray, so originating the phrase 'painting the town red'.

As well as being interested in the prize ring, Waterford was also a keen horseman. In the same year that Perry Fought Freeman, Waterford married Louisa Stuart, daughter of the 1st Baron Stuart de Rothesay, and settled down to a much more sensible life in Curraghmore House in Ireland. He died after a horse riding accident in 1859. Lord George Bentinck (1802–1848) was first a Whig, and later a Conservative, politician and racehorse owner, so he had a lot in common with his companion. It was Waterford who offered to back the 'Tip', as he called him, for a large sum against Caunt, the present champion.

Ben Caunt was behind his counter when these remarks were made, and only sneered, saying that it would be like fighting a mere schoolboy. Perry took the comment to heart and played the schoolboy to mischievous perfection, for he was most keen to obtain the championship. He determined that he would goad Ben into a decision one way or another. The Slasher walked over to the counter, caught hold of the landlord by his handsome black hair, and lifted him bodily over the counter, which led to an immediate struggle. After taking a moment's break, they adjourned to the street where they fought several more rounds. At this the police interfered.

On the following day, Perry, accompanied by the Marquis, took a cab and set off for Tom Springs, where they had heard that Ben was to be found. Tom begged that there might be no repetition of the clash that had happened the day before, and indeed on that occasion there was no further disturbance. The Slasher, however, renewed his challenge and, along with the Marquis, tried to organise a match, but Ben doggedly declined. Subsequently Caunt handed the champion's belt over to Bell's Life and Perry claimed it by default.

The years go by, and we arrive at 1851. That year happened to be an extremely busy one for the Slasher. He travelled the country, worked as an engine fitter, fought Harry Broome – Johnny's brother – and got married to a young lady. I say a young lady, for it was her age that obviously caused a problem. To trace her short lifespan, we need to take a look at the 1841 census. The 1841 census was the first of its kind, though it was expanded at the very next census ten years later. There is precious little detail, but it does give us some pertinent information about the young lady's family, what jobs they held, how old they were and where they lived.

In 1841, the Challingsworth family lived in New Street, Dudley, off Castle Street right in the middle of the town. Of course, Victorian Dudley has pretty much disappeared, but the street layout is almost the same, with a few modern modifications for twentieth-century traffic. In this year, Ann Maria aged six years, was living with her father Edward, forty years of age, and her mother who was thirty. Her father is described as a saddler/innkeeper, while living under the same roof is her older brother William, also a saddler, her older sister Elizabeth, fifteen, brothers George, ten, and James, seven, and younger sister, Zipporah, a fine old bible name.

By the 1851 census, the situation has changed dramatically. Her father had died in his forties and there is no mention of her mother either, though she could have re-married; a lot can happen in ten years. The family has moved to 45 Hall Street, just a few yards away, while the new head of the Challingsworth family is now William, aged thirty, who has married Eliza, aged thirty-one. They are still in the public house business, as William is described as a victualler, while additional clues are in other members of the household.

Ann Maria, now sixteen, is working for her brother as a barmaid, while William already has three children between eight and two years of age. Living in the same building is Thomas Roberts, working as a house servant, William Baldwin is described as a musician from New York, and finally Anne Grainger, a second house servant. We can now imagine the scene of a busy lively inn, serving a noisy and numerous clientele with beer and live music.

How does our famous bare-knuckle fighter get to know this young girl? Of course there is no way to be certain, but it is no stretch of the imagination that he met her while there for a drink, as Victorian Dudley was the nearest town of any size.

Perry was the local hero-cum-celebrity and had travelled widely, whereas the young barmaid had probably never been out of Dudley, and we can easily guess that young Ann Maria was enthralled with this larger than life character who could offer her a much more exciting life than simply sweeping up and cleaning tables. Why, just a few months earlier, on the census previously mentioned, Perry was to be found at a hotel in Coventry describing himself both as an engine fitter but also as a 'Prize Fighter'. At any rate, Perry, who was now almost twice her age – not particularly unusual for that day – wooed her and persuaded her to become his wife. But did he have her family's approval?

Our next piece of information is the marriage certificate of Ann Maria Challingsworth and William Perry. Amongst other small bits of data, it records the marriage taking place in the parish of Pitstone on 11 June. And you may well ask; where is Pitstone? Pitstone was, and still is, a tiny village half way between Leighton Buzzard and Hemel Hempstead, some 16 miles north-east of the outskirts of London in Buckinghamshire. We can only conclude that Perry brought his young lady here to escape her family and get married where no one would ask too many questions.

On the marriage certificate Ann Maria declares her age to be not sixteen, not even seventeen, but the mature age of twenty-two and working as a dressmaker. She was certainly telling lies about her age, and possibly also about her occupation, in order that she could get married. The legal age at the time was twenty-one. Perry signs his name with a cross, showing that, at the age of thirty plus, he had not learned to read or write, though this was not unusual for the time. His wife on the other hand has signed the certificate, showing that she, at least, has had some schooling.

But why choose Pitstone? I think the only clue can be the proximity of Pitstone to the Grand Union Canal, which Perry could easily have been familiar with if he had been employed on long-distance canal-carrying jobs. The canal, a vital link between London and the north, lies less than a mile from the village as it travels south toward the locks and reservoirs at Marsworth. How long the newly-weds stayed at Pitstone no one can say, but Perry certainly finished that eventful year by fighting the younger Harry Broom in October.

The result of that contest was fiercely debated, for in the 15th round a foul was called when Perry hit his opponent when on his knees. In the heat of the battle, no one can claim that this was indeed a despicable deed by the Slasher, but no money changed hands after the fight, and Perry continued to claim that he was the champion, though some would argue that Broome had started out the better man.

I have occasionally wondered why Perry did not have more than one child, for not only did he marry a young wife who stayed with him for the next thirty years, but also, this being the pre-contraceptive era, most families had several children. One answer may be that he did a lot of travelling between his marriage, in 1851, and the running of his first public house, in 1854. Not only did he have his own fights, but he also became the fighting instructor to one Lieutenant J. St Clair Hobson. Elements of the British Army have long had a tradition of boxing and Lieutenant Hobson turned to the Slasher for his training. Unfortunately, Lieutenant Hobson was killed during the Crimean War.

The war in the Crimea was to determine who had authority over the Holy Land, and the empires of Russia, France and Great Britain were flexing their military muscle over territories that once used to be a part of the fading Ottoman Empire. Russia took on the forces of a combined Britain, France and Sardinia, while much of the fighting took place on the Crimean Peninsula.

Lieutenant Hobson was killed during an attack on the Redan, a fortification that protected the town of Sebastopol. After the troops had retreated on the morning of 18 June 1855, Lieutenant W. Hope learned that Lieutenant Hobson was lying outside the trenches badly wounded. He went out to look for him and found him lying in an agricultural ditch running toward the left flank of the Redan.

Finding that Hobson could not be moved without a stretcher, he then ran across open ground under heavy fire from the Russians to get one, and carried it back to where

Hobson was lying. Unfortunately Hobson, of the 7th Regiment of Foot (Royal Fusiliers), was mortally wounded. Lieutenant Hope was awarded the Victoria Cross for his bravery.

By 1854, William Perry, now thirty-five, and his wife, had settled themselves into a public house called The Champions in Spon Lane, West Bromwich. This was no doubt purchased by a combination of his sporting wins and his work as an engine fitter. This latter profession is difficult to define in modern terms, as the internal combustion engine was not yet invented, so Perry may have been working on steam engines which were then utilised in every kind of industry.

Spon Lane, lies on the east side of West Bromwich, and runs south from the High Street and crosses the two Parallel Birmingham canals, known simply as the Old and New Main Lines. The Old Line was built by Brindley in 1772, while the newer and wider Telford Line came fifty years later, to reduce congestion on the former. Three locks lie close to the point where Spon Lane crosses the Old Line, and they are reputedly the oldest set of locks in the Midlands. The pub that Perry owned was only 40-50yds from the canal bridge, and it was here that the couple had their first and, unusual for that era, only child. William Edward Perry was born on 3 December 1854.

The Tipton Slasher had become a father and a retail brewer, an occupation that several pugilists entered on retirement, and one that Perry was to continue in until at least 1861, some four years after losing his last fight to Tom Sayers.

INTO THE BREWING TRADE

From Perry's son's birth certificate of 1854, we see the Slasher working as a retail brewer. He was still in this trade by the 1861 census, though of course by then he had lost his last fight with Tom Sayers and all his money. We know that just after this fight, well wishers, including the Corinthians, had a collection for the defeated Slasher to purchase an alehouse, and this is evidently what he did. By 1861 he was now a licensed victualler and living at 147 Walsall Street, Wolverhampton, not far from the town centre.

Living with him and his wife was his son Edward, now six, and a servant, Mary Walters aged sixteen. It is worth noting that the pub trade of the mid-nineteenth century was not like its modern counterpart. Since the twentieth century, large brewing establishments have taken on the task of making ales and beers. These products are then delivered to the public house in bottles and casks for the landlord to sell. In the nineteenth century, however, the publican or landlord was often responsible for making his own ales and beers.

By the nineteenth century, ale (made from fermented malt) and beer (flavoured with hops) were sold through three main outlets: alehouses, in which the product was brewed on the premises; taverns, which also sold wine; and inns, which provided accommodation. Beer was introduced in the fifteenth century, prior to which ale was the only available drink. Alehouses were initially mostly temporary concerns, run by a local family to supplement their income. However, in the late seventeenth century, their facilities slowly improved and they also began to increase in size. The term public house replaced alehouse in the eighteenth century, and the first purpose-built public houses were erected at the beginning of the nineteenth century.

So, for maybe as long as ten years, Perry produced his own ales and beers. Many years later he admitted that he was never particularly good at business. Whether he meant that he had difficulty managing the financial side of the business or the production of the beer it is impossible to tell. To become a successful publican, Perry needed to do much more than rely on his now fading reputation as a boxer. More importantly, he needed to produce a decent beer that would make his customers come back again and again.

Beer and ale manufacture require an amount of hard work, cleanliness and an aptitude for getting all aspects of the brewing process correct; all this along with workable recipes for ales. Perry's working week was busy, not only attending to customers at the official opening times, but also in preparing the mash and fermentation of the beers. It should be noted that each ingredient can affect flavour, colour, carbonation, alcohol content, and other subtle changes in the beer. Perry lasted until perhaps the mid-1860s as a licensed victualler. After that his life took a turn for the worse, but the Slasher was by no means finished. Work must have been hard to find in the Midlands, so Perry travelled with his wife over 150 miles north of his birth place to the bustling port of Gateshead.

The Fountain Inn, Tipton, 2008. This was Perry's base for some years, though the building did have three stories in those days.

Gateshead, as you may know, sits opposite Newcastle-upon-Tyne on the banks of the River Tyne, one of Britain's busiest rivers. These were the days when the docks were packed with ships, cargoes, sailors and traders. The town really came of age in the 1800s, and the rate of change was staggering. There was massive growth in industry and house building, and the town spread southwards, however this growth was matched in the areas of disease, drunkenness and deprivation.

If the lane to Newcastle was dirty in the 1700s then it was to get a lot dirtier, certainly in the first few decades of the 1800s, after which it started to improve, with lots of new houses being built from the 1860s onwards. Perry was seeking work, and he went back to the trade of his youth – rope-making, which played an important role with all the shipping operating from the quays. Unfortunately, it was at this point that his health deteriorated, and both he and his wife ended up in Gateshead Workhouse.

INTO THE WORKHOUSE

In general, our knowledge of the workhouse is limited to a few ghastly stories from perhaps our grandparents, or maybe we watched Oliver Twist as he begged for more porridge when he was there as a lad. In the nineteenth century, the institution known as the workhouse existed more as a deterrent than a safety net to anyone seeking Government handouts. People only went there when they were truly desperate and they had no one else to help them in their plight.

William and Ann Perry were of this number. There is no way that Perry would have resorted to the workhouse from choice. The illness he suffered from cannot be described in modern technical terms, but was then labelled as a lameness caused by a dropsical affliction connected with hepatic derangement, and was thus labelled so by the medical officer on entering what was commonly and simply called The House. So what was the workhouse really like? Was Gateshead a typical example, and what would the couple have experienced during there stay in it?

In the seventeenth century, Gateshead built a poor house in St Mary's churchyard. Another poor house was acquired in 1750, while others were added over the next eighty years or so. The workhouse rules of 1813 required clean blankets every six months, clean sheets every three weeks, and a daily wash for the inmates. However, by 1838 it was decided that the old buildings were inadequate and that a new workhouse was needed. The site of the new building was at Rectors Field, off what became Union Row, and accommodation for 276 inmates was ready by 13 July 1841. This workhouse was regularly overcrowded, for which the solution was to sleep two inmates to one bed. Small additions to the place were made, including a small sick ward in 1851 (which is probably where Perry went) and a temporary fever hospital in 1866.

William and Ann Perry entered Gateshead Workhouse as a married couple, but there were no provisions for families, and they would have been separated straight away.

Perry's grave, St John's Church, Kates Hill, Dudley.

Children also resided in their own sections, away from their parents. This was just one of the reasons why the 'Spike', as it was called, was rejected by many.

On admission, the pair would first have gone into the receiving ward to await inspection by the medical officer. Their own clothes would have been taken away and cleaned – often fumigated in a stove to kill off any vermin – then stored away with a ticket to be returned on departure. They would have been searched, washed and provided with regulation workhouse attire. Personal objects such as cards, dice and matches would have been confiscated.

One lady recalls being issued, after admission, with two petticoats, a gown and an apron, a pair of stocking legs (without the feet), a pair of carpet shoes (very worn), and one old shift. This would have been a traumatic experience for two people who had been always used to their freedom, and in fact had been their own bosses in the past. Perry would probably have been issued with a coarse blue woollen suit, very probably without underwear.

The workhouse was, by its very nature, occupied by many who were too ill to work, such as Perry was at this time. However, those capable of working could be employed in washing, cleaning, cooking, tending to the gardens, caring for other inmates or doing mindless tasks such as picking oakum.

It is difficult to say what level of care the Perrys received at the hands of the medical officer for, like the house itself, conditions varied enormously from one to another. It often depended upon the personality and style of the guardians, who had ultimate authority, the master and matron, who actually ran the house, and the quality of the medical officer that had been taken on.

The medical men were often young and inexperienced in their duties. They were usually underpaid – which did not encourage the better candidates – and they often had to fund medicines from their own pocket. Then of course there was often friction between the master and the doctor. The master, often being pressured by the guardians to spend as little as possible, may not have been happy to receive instruction from the doctor as to improvements that needed to be made, or perhaps the purchase of bandages and medicines. If the doctor was bad at his job, it was still difficult to get rid of him, as there was often no one else who wanted to take the post. Certainly many people entered the workhouse and never came out alive. A nurse at a workhouse in Paddington relates this story about the death of a female inmate:

> When I went around the ward where she was one afternoon, I observed her pillow had been taken away, and she looked ghastly. I then asked an elderly pauper nurse where the pillow was, and she said, 'She's nearly gone, and I always take the pillows away to make them go quicker, and I have taken her pillow away.' I had the pillow put back immediately, but Ward [the patient] died half an hour later. But at least the inmates got fed!

The Commission – that is to say the Government department that supposedly had the authority over all the workhouses in the country, and the individual board of guardians with its master and matron – had the real authority, and they controlled the food situation. At the heart of the system was the dietary, or menu, that laid down what was to be offered to the paupers at every meal, which included the weight or volume of what was daily dispensed. Foods specified included bread, gruel, meat, broth, cheese, potatoes and rice or suet pudding. Like everything else, the quality of food varied from place to place.

At a workhouse in Bradford, the pauper women rebelled when their cups of tea were replaced with gruel. Three of the ringleaders were brought before the magistrates after refusing to work on that diet and were sent to prison for one week. Certainly at some workhouses, of which there were several hundred throughout the country, the folk inside were tolerably well fed, though Lord Carnarvon did say in 1868 that prisoners often received better food.

We can now ask the question, how long did the Slasher and his wife remain in the workhouse? There is no definite account, but they were certainly in the workhouse during the winter and Christmas of 1869, and back living in the Midlands by the spring census of 1871. My guess is that Perry did not stay in the house for any longer than necessary, and as soon as he was well enough he and Ann would have signed themselves out. Christmas Day in the workhouse may possibly have been the best day of the year for its wretched occupants, but a famous poem of the time by George R. Sims (1847–1922) shows that it was not the cosiest place to be:

It is Christmas day in the workhouse,
And the cold bare walls are bright
With garlands of green and holly,
And the place is a pleasant sight:
For with clear washed hands and faces
In a long and hungry line
The Paupers sit at the tables,
For this is the hour that they dine.

And the guardians and their ladies,
Although the wind is east,
Have come in their furs and wrappers,
To watch their charges feast:
To smile and be condescending,
Put puddings on pauper plates,
To be hosts at the workhouse banquet
They've paid for with their rates.

BACK TO THE BLACK COUNTRY CANALS

So, after maybe a year or more in the Gateshead Workhouse, Perry and his wife make it back to the Black Country, not to Tipton, the famous place of his birth, but to neighbouring Bilston. He was now fifty-two years old, Ann was thirty-nine – now revealing her real age, and their son was aged sixteen. They resided at 22 Ward Street (only a short distance from the Coseley Tunnel). The Slasher had gone from rags to riches to rags and then up a bit. He had obviously recovered from his malady, and stated to the census official that he was now a contractor employing one man; whether that one man was his teenage son or another is open to question.

Yes, Perry was back on the Birmingham canals, back where he started, working in the time-honoured fashion of two men, one horse, and a 70ft boat. He may have purchased a second-hand boat or he could just as easily have rented one, for there were many small operators on the canal network. In his time he had been 'Prize Fighter', fight instructor, rope-maker, engineer, publican, and workhouse inmate.

A man as familiar with the grand rooms of the aristocracy as with the back-to-backs of the poor. Finally, he had returned to operating narrowboats and following the horses' hooves on the grimy waters of the BCN. Acting now as a contractor for the final eight years of his life, he may indeed have been carrying night soil (manure), as has been suggested by others, or he may instead have been carrying coal, as 80 per cent of the rest of the canal operators of the Midlands did.

The Slasher made one more house move before he died (Ann died earlier that same year), to Gibbet Gate, Bilston (renamed Stowe Heath Lane). He was visited during that last week not only by his doctor, but by David Christie Murray, who was a reporter and writer of short novels. Christie Murray was born in West Bromwich, and he was one of the last people to chat with the famous boxer, apart from Perry's son who was present at his father's death. As well as producing several novels, Christie Murray wrote a book entitled *The Makings of a Novelist*, in which he described his last visit to the Slasher:

Statue of William Perry, aka the Tipton Slasher, at Tipton Green.

He was dying when I saw him again, and his vast chest and shoulders were shrunken and bowed so that I wondered where the very framework of the giant had fallen to. He was despised, forgotten and left alone, and he sat on his bed with an aspect altogether rejected and heartless … when I entered the room he was twirling an empty clay tobacco pipe with a weary listless thumb and finger, and the tobacco was welcome. 'They might a let me alon,' he said, when his wit grew clear. 'I 'eld the belt for seventeen 'ear. Tum's a good un. Arv'e sin em all and Arv never sin a better. But he aught to a let me be. There was no credit to be got in ommerin a mon at my time O life. All the same though, I thought I should have trounced him. So I should if I could have got him. Bit he fled hither and thither and walked around me like a cooper around a cask. An I was fool enough to lose me temper, an the crowd began to loff at me, and I took to racing after im. An me wind fairly went, an wheer was I then? E knocked me down fair and square e did. I put everything I ad on that fight and here I am.'

That visit was on Christmas Eve, 1880. Perry was pronounced dead by Dr Cameron on the same day, attended only by his son, with the cause of death being attributed to alcoholism and pulmonary congestion. Though, having said that, Christie Murray reckoned that Perry was certainly not an alcoholic, but had simply been used to drinking his own brew for some time.

As a newspaper report at the time said, it did appear to be a melancholy close to a life of excitement, not to say of wide celebrity status. Since that date, Tiptonians at least have never forgotten their historic hero. For forty years his grave was neglected, until 1925, when a granite slab was placed over it on Kate's Hill Churchyard, Dudley. The *New York Times* ran a small piece that had been taken from the London *Telegraph* which read:

NEW YORK TIMES JANUARY 15TH 1881

Another great hero has quitted the scene of his exploits in the person of Mr Perry, once known as the 'Tipton Slasher'. Into the merits and demerits of prize fighting we do not propose to enter. It had its good aspect possibly; it certainly had its bad side. But the 'Tipton Slasher' was one of those pugilists who did little to bring his occupation or profession into disrepute. It is on record that he fought hard but humanely; that his honesty was undoubted, and that though he eventually succumbed to the superior strength or science of Tom Sayers, he was a skilful and gallant opponent. Following upon the heels of such renowned fighters as Randall, Hudson, Belasco, Martin, Cribb and Spring, he yet belonged to the class which considered that a fair and straightforward fight was a creditable and satisfactory performance. He and his friends at any rate held the knife and revolver in abhorrence, contending that the fist was the most natural weapon and that by its aid disputes should be settled. That class of men seems to have died out, and it is for those who make the manners, customs and ethics of peoples their peculiar study to determine whether its disappearance is a gain or a loss to the nation.

12

HETTY SEYMOUR AND THE SEVERN & CANAL CARRYING COMPANY

Today, the inland waterways are filled with leisure craft and very few working boats. However, fifty years ago, the river and canal system formed an important part of the transport economy of Britain. Several large fleets of boats did the bulk of the carrying, while many smaller concerns with just one or two boats did the remainder.

Hetty's parents were working for one of the larger fleets, the Severn & Canal Carrying Company, when she was born in 1936. Her father, William Albert Helm, came from a dynasty of boaters; however, her mother, Kate, came 'off the bank', as they used to refer to people who lived in houses rather than on a boat. This was the period between the wars, and boat carrying had seen a downturn since the First World War when much work had gone to the motor lorry.

The River Severn had been an important artery for a thousand years, but saw a rise in prosperity after the opening of the Staffordshire & Worcestershire Canal in 1772, and later when the Worcester & Birmingham Canal opened in 1815. The latter did take some trade from the former, because it was a shorter route to Worcester. During earlier centuries, the Severn had suffered from navigational difficulties. However, after receiving many improvements and the building of strategic locks, the river and the inland towns of Worcester and Stourport continued to be important ports through the nineteenth and the first half of the twentieth century.

The Severn & Canal Carrying, Shipping & Steam Towing Company had been formed as far back as 1874 from two former companies. They operated six trows, six lighters, four tugs and about fifty narrowboats. Later, after some changes to the company, they leased or owned warehouses at Gloucester (which was their administrative base), Worcester, Bristol, Stourport (where they had a dock and workshops) and Gas Street, Birmingham. Their larger river boats also called at Avonmouth and the South Wales ports.

George Cadbury controlled the company in the early years of the twentieth century. The narrowboats were timber and pulled by tugs on the river, and by horses or mules on the canal sections. In 1927, the company purchased the first of their motor boats from the Anderton Company. The first batch were Bollinder-powered, and at first they were fitted to previous horse-boats. Just before Hetty was born, however, the company

Left: Hetty Seymour with her boat at New Bridge, Wolverhampton, 2007.

Below: Gloucester Lock in the 1950s. Severn & Canal Carrying Company were based here.

had eight iron boats built to take Petter engines. This next section is Hetty's account of the last flourish of the narrowboat carrying trade.

HETTY SEYMOUR

My mother and father had two 70ft boats, the *Oak* and the *Ash*. They were built by Charles Hill & Sons of Bristol and registered in Gloucester in 1934. So, when I and my five brothers and sisters came along, the boats were almost new. They were powered by 9hp Petters which came with forward and reverse gears. Similar boats included the *Elm*, *Fir*, *Pine*, *Willow*, *Beech* and *Alder*. This engine could cope with motoring up the Severn to either Worcester or Stourport, unless the Severn was travelling faster than usual.

These boats did not carry as much weight as the horse-boats, but they did go faster. The horse-boats had to be tied together to be towed up the river by the larger tugs. It took about six to seven hours from Gloucester to Worcester, where we then went though Diglis Lock and on to the still waters of the Worcester & Birmingham Canal. From that point it was locks all the way to the Birmingham summit at Tardebigge; another fourteen to sixteen hours of almost solid lock wheeling for us growing kids. After that it was level cruising all the way through Wast Hill Tunnel and on to Birmingham. I was the second oldest child, Kathleen was older than me, but she was a sick child – today we call it cerebral palsy.

Thus, as effectively the eldest, I had the responsibility of taking the younger ones with me wherever I went. We all slept in the one cabin, as Dad did not want to lose any of us going into the water at night. The two youngest slept underneath Mom and Dad's bed. My parents were wonderful; strict, but kind too. Most nights Dad would get us all singing the old songs, while Mom sang along with an excellent voice. Dad played all of the tunes on his harmonica and he taught me how to play. Dad did not read or write, but because Mom came off the bank she did, and she tried to educate us with simple reading books when she had the time. But there was not much free time, as we were either boating from one place to another, loading and unloading or sheeting up the holds. In between, there was just time to keep the boat clean and do the cooking. We did go to the cinema from time to time, and that was a real treat.

I recall one Christmas what we kids were given. We each had a banana, one apple and an orange. I had a Pattern Pam book, which contained cardboard cut-outs of ladies. I used to spend ages cutting out the different clothes for them to wear. John had a colouring book, Henry had a teddy, while Maureen and Dianne had small dolls. I never felt that we went without, though Dad could be a bit miserable if he did not get sugar in his tea. I remember we tried sweetened milk and even golden syrup on a couple of occasions. Often it would be cups of tea for us out of a used jam jar without the luxury of sugar. Rabbit stew was regularly on the menu, but I cannot remember how Dad came by them. I know he often caught eels from somewhere on the Worcester & Birmingham Canal, which he skinned and then fried.

Sharpness in the 1950s was a regular port of call for the Severner's.

Our family cabin was toward the rear of the boat, in front of the engine bay; it was about 10ft long. It contained a double bed that could be folded away during the daytime, and one large cupboard that had a fold-down door which became our dining table. Dad was pretty strict about meals, and we generally ate at the table and had to ask to leave it. We had a small coal-fired range for heating and cooking. Drinking water was kept in the large can on the roof, topped up from a variety of points. We carried all sorts of cargoes such as sugar, tea, cheese; canned foods like tomatoes, all kinds of metals, and barrels of stuff called carbide.

My favourite cargo came from the Cadbury's factories at Bourneville or Frampton, where we loaded up with a kind of raw chocolate that was called crumb. Crumb looked a bit like putty, but not only was it good to eat but us kids sold small lumps of it to others for a few pence. The crumb was loaded in large sacks that had to be carefully stacked in the hold. At Bourneville, Cadbury's had a toyshop for the children to play in while the adults got on with unloading sugar from the boats. We loaded up with chocolate mass from Bourneville; this was also pretty good to eat.

When I was just a youngster, the war came along. This brought more work than usual to the inland waterways. Due to the heavy bombing of London and the coastal vessels in the Channel around Dover, the Government moved a lot of transport to the west coast and up the River Severn. Now, not only were we carrying the usual kinds of goods, but also stuff for the war effort such as shells and bomb cases.

Hetty aged eighteen with her mother Kate, *c.*1954. BW boats the *John* and *Ferret* en route to the Anderton lift and Weston Point.

Dennis Beck and Hetty with the butty *Kidsgrove* — *Trout* is off picture, 1959.

None of our boats were ever hit due to bombing, but it was a close call for us on a couple of occasions. First, when we were shot at by a Jerry plane while on the Severn, and once one night in the centre of Birmingham. As soon as the sirens had gone off, a man came and knocked on the cabin side and told us to get quickly in to the shelters. However, on the way a warden turned us back and told us that the shelter had been hit. We spent the rest of the raid underneath Gas Street Tunnel.

Even though the canals and the narrowboat fleets had carried over a million tons of cargo during the war years, the work was to slack off after 1945. In 1947, the inland waterways were nationalised. At first it was the British Transport Commission, while later on British Waterways came into being, with their blue and white colour schemes. Following that, the old method of boats being constantly gauged and paying tolls was replaced by a yearly license.

As well as the hazards due to the war, the canal itself was always a source of danger too. We were going down the Wolverhampton 21 at 4a.m. on one occasion, heading for Aldersley Junction where boaters often moored. It was while we were in one of the locks that I discovered a body. Dad sent for the police, who told us off for not getting the body out; but it is not easy to get a heavy water-sodden body out of a lock.

Mrs Jinx with the *Kidsgrove*; Harry Powel on the towpath, Barbridge.

On another day, as we came out of Wolverhampton Top Lock, I saw a small boy go in to the water then a girl jumped in to save him. I reversed back to help, grabbing the pole from the roof to try and pull one of them out. Fortunately the men from the railway yard were about and they managed to get the boy out safe, but sadly the girl drowned.

The Severn is a beautiful river, but it could also be a tricky water to navigate, either going up or down it. The one at the helm always tried to keep the boat on the inside of the bends, so as to stay in the slack water. I saw a boat break from its moorings near Stourport one day and break in two as it hit the weir. Our worst tragedy, however, involved my sister Dianne, who was crushed in the lock gate at Stone. I still remember how she screamed today.

The company were very good to us, and allowed my family to keep the boat moored at Stoke-on-Trent for two years while she was in the hospital. I found a job working at one of the Potbanks, where they made cups and saucers, while Dad and John got a job on the locks. I was fifteen and it was my first real job. I would take a small piece of clay, pat and roll it in my hand before pushing it into a mould. After pressing it well in with my thumb, the mould went off to the machine which formed it into a cup. Workers were often tested to see if they had 'potters rot'. This was a lung complaint and came from working with powdered china clay for too long. Unfortunately, Dianne never recovered, and she died of pneumonia at the end of those two years. We went back to the canal.

I married Dennis Beck when I was twenty-one years old. He worked for British Waterways and I transferred on to the *Trout*, our first boat, though later we also had the *John* and the *Ferret*. Cargoes and routes changed, and we sometimes went to Gloucester or Manchester Docks. Here we loaded up from enormous ships with spelter and copper, which often came down to Sherborne St in Birmingham.

In the early days, boats used to be pulled through the Harecastle Tunnel by a tug, but after the tug went you chugged through the darkness under your own engine power. The fumes inside the tunnel could be pretty bad, so they installed a huge fan at one end that pulled the air through. That was a small improvement. One day, when we were near Red Bull, I fell in with my overcoat and wellies on. Dennis did not notice me go in, and it took all my strength to pull myself out. I was so exhausted and my nails were ruined; I just lay there on the towpath for a while until I got my breath back. Bringing up three children on the boat was also a challenge. When they were small we used short reins to secure them to the boat. This was the usual way that boating parents kept their children from falling in.

In 1961, I left the canals. For many years I never went near them, but then I took a couple of short boating holidays and realised how much I missed them. I did a little bit of boating work for Ron Gregory Cruisers, near Wolverhampton, taking school trips to Brewood or Middlewich. Later, I bought my own small 30-footer, *Kitty*, and now in my seventies, along with my brother John, we spend as much time as possible touring the waterways together.

13

ALBERT BRACE

The well-known canal-carrying company started by James Fellows had been plying the waterways for almost one hundred years when I was born in 1934. Though his original dock had been at Tipton on the BCN, the company had grown considerably since those early days. Between the wars, Fellows, Morton & Clayton were operating from several bases around the country. Fazeley Street, Birmingham, is perhaps their most well-known depot, and we were there often.

I, however, was born on the narrowboat *Kilsby* to Jack and Eliza Brace at the Bordesley Street Depot in Birmingham. Here, the company had the use of a basin plus warehousing facilities. This depot was not far from the bottom of the Ashted Locks, half a mile west of Bordesley Junction, while the company's boat-building and repair dock was a mile away at Saltley on the Grand Union Canal.

I had two brothers, Jack and Isaac, and a sister Violet. All of us learned the ways of the canals as we grew up. *Kilsby* was our butty boat; the iron motor was *Pilot*, built in 1924 at Saltley and registered in Birmingham. However, boat people were always moving from one boat to another, always trying to find one in a better condition or maybe with a little more room, so we transferred to the motor *Nautilus*, built at Northwich, and the butty *Egypt*. Later on we were to have the motor *Erica* with the butty *Fay*.

Most carrying companies used a variety of engines, but Fellows, Morton & Clayton were loyal Bollinder users. It was just prior to the First World War that the company tested one of the new Swedish Bollinder engines, and the *Linda*, built at Saltley, was fitted out with a 15hp version. When I worked for the company, 15hp engines were used on the motors that had a butty and 9hp engines were fitted to the single motors. In the past, Fellows, Morton & Clayton had used several steamers, but all had been converted to Bollinders in my day.

When I look back on the years spent as a youngster, I remember the beautiful hot summers that we used to have in those days, and working through endless numbers of locks. The Grand Union was well blessed with lock flights, and during hot dry spells as we worked our way toward Tring Summit, there always appeared to be water shortages. So, we would moor up for a day or so between Northchurch and Cowroast and wait for water levels to rise.

Albert Brace with Matty's tug *Pacific* dredging in 1981.

During the war years we would be issued with ration books like every one else. These little books, full of coupons, could be used in a limited number of shops along the canal to purchase weighed portions of tea, sugar, cheese etc., so even though food was limited we did not do too badly. And the whole family knew their routine for work. Dad or my older brother steered the motor, Mom the butty, while the rest of us lock wheeled. Occasionally I had a day at school at Bulls Bridge, but that was a rarity, and I was not able to read or write until I was much older.

During the Second World War, London was always the prime target for German bombers, but Birmingham was also attacked, and one night Fellows, Morton & Clayton's depot at Warwick Wharf was bombed. Though the building took a direct hit and several boats were sunk, no crew were hurt. The canal was also breached for a while.

We carried all kinds of goods in those days; foodstuffs like sugar and tea, while the next day you could be loading up with metals such as copper or lead. We would load up at a number of wharfs in the Birmingham area and then spend four or five days travelling down the Grand Union to City Road, London. Once or twice we went over to Stewarts & Lloyds at Coombs Wood on the Dudley No.2 canal. Stewarts & Lloyds made steel tubes and though they had their own boats, they tended to stick to short-haul traffic, while Fellows, Morton and Clayton did the long runs.

In his book on Fellows, Morton & Clayton, Alan Faulkner describes one of these runs with the boats *Admiral* and *Upton*. After loading with tubes at Coombs Wood and staying the night at Fazeley Street, the pair travelled to Brentford in seventy-two hours; a journey of 149 miles and 176 locks – quite a feat.

When I was fifteen, Dad died and mother took over as skipper with help from my step-brother Alf, as Dad had been married before. We went on the cement run for a month or two, boating from Southam, near Long Itchington on the Grand Union, up to Sampson Road, Birmingham. This was a very tight schedule of three runs each week. On Monday morning we would load up with bags of cement at Southam Works at 9a.m., and arrive finally near Sampson Road at about 1a.m. the next day. The next day we got up 6a.m., ready to get unloaded. The only time we were not boating, loading or unloading was Saturday afternoon. I remained with Mom for another two years.

All this happened at roughly the same time as the waterways were being nationalised, and what had been Fellows, Morton & Clayton became British Waterways. Out were the old red cabins with white lettering, and in was the new blue and yellow of the nationalised industry. Re-painting and lettering of the fleet took place generally at Bulls Bridge, Uxbridge and Saltley.

Arriving at the important and pivotal age of eighteen was the gateway to boating opportunities. At that age I was old enough to go on my own, and I took charge of the *Lion* and the *Grange*. I now steered and operated the motor, while Mom and Violet were behind on the butty. Violet was a great help; she used her bike for lock wheeling and assisted with the cooking.

Braunston was a busy junction in those days; situated on the main route between Birmingham and London and the route up the Coventry Canal toward the Trent & Mersey. Fellows, Morton & Clayton had an important base there, as had Pickford's before them, but it had also been the home of Nurser's Boat Building and the Samuel Barlow Coal Company who followed them. The latter had important coal-carrying contracts between the productive coal fields north of Coventry and large canal-based industries at the southern end of the Grand Union. I went as captain for them. At that date I reckon they were operating around a dozen pairs of boats that included the *Prince* and *Stirling Castle*. I took on the motor *Alec*, with its twin-cylinder Lister engine, and my brother Ike steered the butty *Montgomery*. The man who gave us our orders at Braunston was Bob McDonald.

Just as Fellows, Morton & Clayton boats were referred to as 'Joshers', Samuel Barlow's was know as the 'Limited' to distinguish it from S.E. Barlow's that operated from Glascote, near Tamworth. S.E. Barlow was started by the grandson of the original Samuel Barlow, and it was eventually taken over by the older company in 1957 when coal contracts were dwindling generally.

Though dedicated coal boats, Barlow's operated some of the most beautifully painted and decorated boats on the waterways at that time. The main cabin panel was a dark glossy green with white lettering. This panel was surrounded with a grained border, next to which on the butties was a large castle. The ram's head and tiller were also colourfully decorated, while the name of the boat was written in large white letters on a red background at the rear.

Several East Midland collieries were strung out along the Coventry Canal, and they included the ones at Bedworth (Newdigate Colliery), Longford, Griff and Baddesley. The Coventry Canal between Braunston and Rugby wanders gently between the borders of Warwickshire and Northamptonshire, though its route is many miles shorter than the original eighteenth-century version. In the very early days, the Coventry Canal meandered left and right, adding unnecessarily to the journey, however Cubitt's improved route had cut off many of the loops, thus introducing a succession of aqueducts, cuttings and embankments. These we were to become intimately familiar with after each passing week.

The collieries had their own individual ways of loading the boats. At Bedworth and Baddesley, coal was shovelled straight out of railway trucks into the holds, while at others, the coal dropped out of steel hoppers. Baddesley Basin was a short arm and the coal was delivered by railway, as the pit was some distance away. The basin was surrounded by fields, with only a pub and a few cottages for company. A small polished steam engine took away the empty trucks and delivered full ones right next to us on the wharf. After manoeuvring the boat next to the trucks, a worker at the wharf knocked the catches from the truck door, allowing tons of coal to stream into the boat. *Alec* and *Montgomery* would then sink gently down into the water as each truck was emptied until there was just enough freeboard to keep them afloat. The pair of boats carried 50 tons between them; 27 tons in the butty and 23 tons in the motor.

After loading, we were off south towards Milton Keynes and Leyton Buzzard, to one of many destinations along the Grand Union. We never took coal north into Birmingham, those contracts had finished years before. John Dickinson's paper mills took regular boatloads; the company and its wharf were right on the canal side at Frogmore, not far from Hemel Hempstead. We were paid an extra £6 for emptying out the boats.

A couple of miles further south was Kings Langley, where we took coal to the Ovalteen Works. There was always the wonderful smell of chocolate in the air along this stretch of the waterway as the company manufactured its famous bed-time drink. Other coal drops included the Nestles Cocoa Factory, just north of Bulls Bridge, but probably the most unusually titled factory belonged to the jam manufacturers Kearley & Tonge's. Boat trips to this destination were nicknamed the 'Jam Ole Run'. At Kearley & Tonge's the company had a skip that they lowered into the boat; they also had their own men to empty out. At Ovalteen they operated a grab for removing the coal.

I will just make a point about working hours at this stage. Everyone employed by Barlow's got paid at the end of the trip – ignoring start-out money of course. This meant that you could work as many hours as you liked, within reason; workers were just as interested in earning as much as possible in those days as they are today. Some boaters started at 4a.m. and worked right through to 10p.m. That was far more than Ike and I were prepared to do, and we stuck to a less demanding routine. We commenced at 5 or 6a.m. and tied up ten or twelve hours later. At least this arrangement gave us some time to ourselves. We were young single men and we reckoned that we earned enough.

I left Barlow's in 1956 and went to live with my brother, Jack, for a while on the land in Wolverhampton. During that time I had a job working for British Rail, right next to the Wolverhampton 21 locks. Every day I watched the boats going up and down the locks, and in the end it all became a bit too much. I decided that I needed to go back to the cut. Once a boatman always a boatman, it seemed.

Albert Brace, 2005.

Just South of Wolverhampton on the Main Line Canal, near Coseley, was the firm of Alfred Matty & Sons. I went to work for them along with Jim Moore, who later became my brother-in-law, and Bill Tolly senior. So, the next morning we set off at 5a.m. Bill Tolly had the tug, Jim steered the next two day boats, while I followed up in the rear as we set out for the pits situated along the Cannock Extension Canal just off the Wyrley & Essington Canal.

Jim was always a bit of a practical joker, and on the way over in the dark he threatened to cut me adrift if I made a noise. Sure enough, at Lane Head he did just that, and I had to bowhaul until I caught up with the tug. We delivered that first load of coal to Wrights Forge in Tipton, not far from The Fountain Inn. The forge has of course long gone and been redeveloped as the Neptune Health Centre. After that, we picked up a few empties and headed back to the pits at Brownhills. This was our routine about three times each week.

Destinations for coal deliveries were the foundries and factories around the Black Country, and occasionally Stewarts & Lloyds, near Netherton. As coal carrying came to a close I then went on to boat rubbish away from Albright & Wilson's in Oldbury using the *Maureen*. This was a regular contract for many years, getting rid of phosphorous waste.

Matty's had a lot of contracts for dredging in those days, so it was inevitable that I moved on to that rather un-glamorous aspect of canal maintenance. At first we used the spoon dredger, which was truly hard manual work for the three-man crew, but fortunately we went mechanised with a hydraulic grab. Over the next two decades, before retirement, I think that I must have dredged nearly every inch of the Midlands canals – and some places several times over. Chance's Basin, near West Bromwich, was a regular trouble spot, with Chillington Wharf, near Wolverhampton, a second, but the Round Oak Steel Works was one of the worst places to silt up.

The Round Oak was an enormous steel works next to Brierley Hill (it has long been demolished and replaced by the Merry Hill Shopping Centre). The steel works extracted water from the canal and returned it full of muck. As you can imagine this was not one of our favourite locations, but Matty's made money from doing some very dirty jobs. To access the Dudley Canal we occasionally used to go through the old Dudley Tunnel, hauled along by the tug *Electra*. Then, about 1970, I was on the television for a few brief moments after the ATV cameras came along to do a bit of filming. They set their crew on the towpath as I went passed on the *Governor*.

Another challenge during that period was dredging the Stourbridge Arm. When boating along that stretch today, it is hard to imagine what a reedy swamp that arm was back in the 1980s. Today, the whole stretch is a tribute to all the hard work from many parties that have campaigned and struggled to open the canals for the leisure industry.

One of the last places I dredged before retirement was the Ashwood Marina. In the past this had been a dirty coal wharf on the Staffordshire & Worcestershire Canal, just below Swindon. Today it is a very pretty location, used for the long-term mooring of colourful leisure boats. Certainly the waterways have changed tremendously since my birth on the Fellows, Morton & Clayton butty back in 1934.

14

HORACE FOSTER

A DAY IN THE LIFE OF A BCN BOATMAN

It is true to say that the numbers of old boatmen – and women for that matter – are dwindling with the passing of each year. So, it was with great pleasure that I came across Horace Foster at the boating festival at Parkhead, near Dudley, in September of 2008. Following an extremely wet summer, the Parkhead festival of 2008 was blessed with fine weather – well, at least the Saturday was – and Horace, known just as H by his friends, was sitting comfortably in the sunshine next to a particularly attractive boat *Jjinad*.

After chatting for a short while, H suggested that on the Monday immediately after the boat gathering, it might be interesting to re-enact one of his BCN boating trips from the old days; the old days being the 1960s, that is. He would steer his boat, his nephew, Gareth, would do the lock wheeling, while Horace and I would stand on the traditional counter of *Mayflower* and generally chat the hours away.

Like other boat people, and especially those from the Black Country, H has the vocabulary of that genre, which means that some of his phrases and terminology are peculiar to those who worked the boats of that era. Therefore it was interesting to hear him talk of 'Oss fettlers' and being 'stemmed up'. They also had their own description of canal locations which does not always tally with the modern labels.

During the later 1950s and early 1960s, Horace worked for T.S. Element. This was one of the well-known boat companies working the Birmingham Canal system, and Horace was at least the third generation. His grandfather, Thomas, was a boatman for Ernie Thomas, another well-known medium-sized canal carrier. Horace's grandmother, Annie (who was born on a boat), worked alongside her husband. Horace's father, Charlie, also worked for Elements, though he had boated for other companies such as S. Barlow's and British Waterways in the past.

So, at Element's, Charlie and Horace were a father and son team, one of several in the firm. Horace's uncle, Horace James, and his brother, William, were also boatmen, so as you can see it was a family affair. Element's operated from two boat yards, one at Oldbury, which tended to take care of the coal boating on the Staffordshire & Worcestershire Canal, and the main site at Salford, where Horace and his father were based.

Perry Bar Lock 13 – known as Gills by the boatmen. H and his father are bringing the *Princess Anne* (small Woolwich with a Gardiner) away from Salford Junction on the way to Anglesey basin, 1966.

Salford, as you may know, is the four-way canal junction at the north of Birmingham that now sits uncomfortably under Spaghetti Junction. George Element was the boss in those days, and he was known for driving around in his Vauxhall Cresta, checking up on the progress of his men and boats. Bill Stevens was the yard foreman, and he was known as a horse fettler. It was Bill's job to look after the stables, mix the horse feed, care for the tack, and generally do any odd jobs around the yard such as empty the rainwater out of the boats when required.

Other boatmen included Dicky Parkin, Albert Rook, Tom Plant and his son, Freddy Hadley and Tom Micklewright. Element's horse-boats, with green cabins and red panels, included the *Coronation, Ernest, George, Walter, Iris, James, Charles, Betty* and *Martha*, mostly named after Element's family members; at least I do not think they had a child called Coronation.

When I asked H exactly what run he fancied doing, he initially recalled the regular runs down the Coventry Canal to the coal fields there, but decided that that was out of the way, so in the end we settled on performing two smaller runs within the confines of the BCN. H recalled:

We used to boat rubbish regularly away from Bellis & Morcom, or Davenports Brewery. Davenports was off what we called Salvage Turn – at the start of the Worcester & Birmingham Canal, while Bellis & Morcom were on the Icknield Port Loop.

So, we commenced our BCN boating day from the centre of Birmingham, boating past Gas Street Basin and onto the Birmingham to Wolverhampton Main Line. This would be the easy part of the journey; no locks and easy water. Things were to get a little rougher as we came to what Horace termed the 'bottom pound'. After just over two and a half hours, we arrived at West Bromwich and turned right at Pudding Green Junction, entering the Walsall Canal.

After a few more bends we were at Ryder's Green top lock, and ready to go down 'The Eight'. So, into the first lock we went, and I decided to time the descent. Seven of the Ryder's Green locks are pretty close together and bring you to Great Bridge, while the eighth is at the end of a slightly longer pound. The time was 9.25a.m. The original trip could have been accomplished by Element's either with a horse-boat, or later by a motor and butty; we were of course only going to pretend, and so we were going to use H's present motor boat, *Mayflower*, named after one of Element's boats.

Above left: Horace with a sack of corn on his back and Betty at Walsall Top Lock, *c.*1966.

Above right: Descending the Ryder's Flight of locks toward Great Bridge, September 2008.

A horse-drawn coal boat going through Great Bridge in the 1960s and past the entrance to what was the Haines Branch. (D .Wilson)

Horace and his father were unusual in the fact that, almost as soon as the working boats finished, they bought their own. They just could not envision a life not connected to the waterways. H has had *Mayflower* for some twenty years, but along with his father they have owned the *Vulcan*, which had previously been a steamer with Fellows, Morton & Clayton, *Falcon*, a Great Western boat, *Norwind*, an ex-Josher, and their last and present boat, *Mayflower*, powered by a Lister. We came out of Ryder's bottom lock at 10.20a.m., almost an hour for The Eight. I asked H if this was slow, as I had an idea that it was. After a moment's thought, he said:

We would have done the Ryder's Flight in maybe half to three quarters of an hour with a horse boat. Though it could easily have taken that long with a motor and butty, because you would have had to bow haul the butty through the locks. In the old days I would have strapped the lock gate as we came in, and used the paddles to get a bit of a helping hand. If it had been a horse-boat, we would have used a pulley off the main mast to help the horse get a good start – not the sort of practice that we use today. Of course in those days the Cut Copper might have caught you doing something wrong and then you would have been in trouble. 'The Cut Copper?' I asked.

Yes, there was Joe the Cut Copper, employed by the Canal Company to make sure that the boatmen behaved themselves. In years past it was a trespassing offence for any one other than a working boatman to go on the towpath. You just couldn't go for stroll along the towpath like you do today – it was well known to be Private Property and there were signs to tell you that.

'What was your father like?' I asked, as we motored away past the Tame Valley Junction. We were now on the infamous bottom pound and expecting trouble. H had his mobile phone ready to call British Waterways if necessary.

Dad was known as a real gentleman. He stayed with the horse-boats right to the end in 1961. We would catch the last bus from Walsall to Aston at 11.45p.m., and then transfer to an electric tram to Salford. The trams ran all night. We would arrive at the depot between 1 and 2a.m., and make sure that the horse had had a good feed. Then we would make our way with an empty boat to the coal pit at Pooley Hall near Tamworth on the Coventry Canal. Once at Pooley Hall, we would swap over to one of the waiting full boats, taking our helm, tiller, mast and coats with us. Not forgetting of course the most important items – the stove, frying pan and tea pot. If you were careful, you could lift out the stove and place it in the next boat with the fire still going. At Pooley Hall, boats were loaded from rail trucks. Every pit had its own way of loading. After 1961, our first motor boat was the *Princess Anne*. Dad steered the motor, while I had the butty.

As H predicted, the going after the Tame Valley Junction did get a little bit harder. I noticed that the tiller was vibrating; H said that we were hitting the silt at the bottom.

Of course, it is a catch-22 situation: British Waterways will not fund expensive dredging if only two or three boats come this way during a year, and many boaters will not come to the Walsall Canal if the dredging is not done. We hit a few objects whilst going through bridge holes. There was a bit of a scrape and a rumble as the boat went over a shopping trolley, or some other metallic object. 'I shall have to clear the prop off later,' said H.

The conversation then shifted naturally to the Parkhead Boat Show from the previous weekend. We all admitted that it had been a wonderful event, and I said that it was always good to have a horse-boat on display. 'Yeah, but they don't operate the osses like in the old days,' declared H. 'What do you mean?' I enquired?

Charlie Foster on the Elements boat *Princess Anne*.

Well, they keep the oss at the lock for a start. If you was taking a boat down the locks, you wouldn't keep the oss at the lock, he would naturally go to the end of the line and wait there; that's if it had been trained well. Also you would always have blinkers on an oss. Osses shy at the most unlikely time, and even at small noises, so you need to keep 'em blinkered, otherwise you might have yer oss go in the cut. We had that happen once going in to Birmingham. Rain had flooded down the embankment onto the towpath, and there was a lot of mud about. The horse struggled and fell and eventually went in the canal. We called the Fire Brigade out, but instead of walking him to a suitable place, they used one of those cradles. Eventually they lifted him out.

By this time we were at Moxley, where Ernie Thomas used to have his tip. This was the end of the first half of our reconstruction. Now we would imagine that we left our rubbish boat to be emptied by the old steam crane, pick up another empty, and head for our final destination, Anglesey Wharf. At that point we would leave our empty boat – the end of a boating day. Sometimes, when ashes were part of the rubbish for disposal, they were used to repair towpaths.

Anglesey Wharf was just one of the sites in the Brownhills area where coal was still being mined in the 1960s. We could just as easily have been taking the empty boat to one of the pits along the Cannock Extension Canal, or even right up to Hednesford Basin – now no longer reachable. As we cruised slowly around the Walsall Canal, H pointed out where some of the old works had been such as Richards Basin, where Clayton's used to load up with tar or creosote, and Bradley & Foster's. Sadly, the new A4444 has robbed the Walsall Canal of much of its old charm and interest, and it is difficult to see where many of the old basins and junctions went away from the main line.

We reached Walsall and the bottom lock of the Walsall Eight by 1.10p.m. The old flour mill, next to the ring road and lock seven, has been revamped for modern accommodation, and there were some very posh apartments included in the same development. At the top lock we halted for at least half an hour while H and Gareth partook of a pint or two from the Navigation pub. It makes one wonder how much longer some of these old canal pubs will remain open. At the moment, five pubs each day are being closed in Britain, quite a radical change in the architectural landscape.

The house that Ernie Thomas once lived in is still there next to the top lock, and H told me that Ernie's house used to have a small arm leading off the canal into Ernie's personal boat house. We turned right at Birchills Junction, and by 4p.m. we were passing through Little Bloxwich. 'We got iced up once on the Dow (Daw) End Branch,' said H, threading the boat through a bridge hole.

We had to wait until the ice boat came through to make a way. Usually ice boats were pulled by horses, but on that occasion it was pulled by a tractor.

According to my calculations, we had done 11 miles from Ryder's Green Junction to Little Bloxwich in six and a half hours, well under the 2 miles per hour average. Of course, we had stopped for half an hour, but this would have been the same as swapping boats at Moxley Tip. Added to that were the 6.5 miles from Birmingham to Ryder's; a total so far of 17.5 miles, and still another 6.5 to do. We should have been at our penultimate destination, Anglesey Basin, by 7p.m.

Once at the basin, H would have swapped over to a loaded boat, and then taken that a short way to Harry's Wharf at Freeth Bridge. Only after stabling and feeding the horse would it have been time to catch the bus home. The grand total would have been approximately 25 miles and 16 locks of boating in about thirteen to fourteen hours of work; about an average day for a BCN boatman.

Ascending the Walsall Locks with the redeveloped Flour Mill to the rear. The mill had a small basin where the FMC boats used to unload.

15

THE BCN CRUISE, SEPTEMBER 2008

Not every year, but as often as it can be arranged, members of the BCN Society organise a cruise around as much of the Birmingham canals as possible. During the summer of 2008, I joined Brian and Brenda Ward on their narrowboat, *Colehurst*, to check out the state of the said navigations. The purpose of the cruise has at least three aims; one, to introduce new boaters to the wonders of the BCN and escort them around in the safety of a small convoy; two, to ensure that some less-frequented parts of the BCN get to see at least a few boats plying their waters; and three, it is good to give these important waterways continual consideration, lest something ill befall them.

At this point I would like to mention volunteers. Volunteers are, in many ways, the lifeblood of the waterways. Yes, British Waterways are the professionals, but it is the volunteers that carry the passion forward. Brian and Brenda are typical of our canal volunteers, and Brenda, now the editor of the BCNS magazine *Boundary Post* for the last four years, does a marvellous job of running the society's magazine.

Boats from all around the country arrived at Cambrian Wharf, Birmingham, for the start of the week's cruise. It was one of those grey days that were common in the August of that year, but there was no dampening of the desire to get out and experience what the BCN had to offer. The objective of the first day was to take the route out of Birmingham toward Wolverhampton, and explore some of the old loops that were created by the Telford developments of the 1820s.

Those of you who are familiar with the BCN will know that Telford came along in 1824 to make some rather important improvements to the older wandering Brindley Cut. In doing so, he created several loops that, during the nineteenth century, became little hives of industry. Often, the factory owners built right up to the waterway wall, forming narrow canyons. At other times they built their own wharfs so that boats could bring in coal and other raw materials, and then boat out the finished goods.

Of course that world has pretty much disappeared; that is why I urge you to come, see and photograph this industrial environment before it goes. Ray Shill has done a marvellous job of researching the local industries, but it is a fine thing to see it oneself and then read about it in a book. Within a few years, that is the only place that you will find it – in a book. I recall the words of Michael Pearson in his guide to the BCN some

Left: Alan Veness leaving the Birmingham 13 behind.

Below: Brenda Ward of the BCNS starts to organise the 2008 cruise from Cambrian Warf.

years ago, when he wrote that he feared for the BCN, and encouraged people to visit it before the planners sanitised it into oblivion.

We boated past Farmers Bridge top lock under the benign gaze of the BT Tower and the indoor arena. Almost straight away we entered the first of those loops and coasted slowly past Sherborne Wharf. Fellows, Morton & Clayton once had their offices here, but now – like most decent old buildings – it has been converted. Also overlooking the loop are the new posh kind of apartments that only the well-heeled can afford. Boats lined the canal, while a wonderfully narrow, dark, old bridge provided the entrance. It was equipped with two little red doors that were provided during the Second World War for access for the Fire Brigade. The doors did not have their rollers, but we did come across some that did later in the day.

By now, we were a little convoy of around eight boats. The others were going to explore the Engine Arm by going up the Smethwick Locks and across Telford's superb Engine Arm Aqueduct. At the end of that arm are good boating facilities and a winding place. *Colehurst* then entered the Icknield Port Loop, which as you may know has no towpath. In the old days, boats needed to punt their way around if they did not have an engine.

This loop is still important for several reasons. Firstly, it butts up to the Rotten Park Reservoir, where much of the water for the BCN is kept, and the feeder is located at one corner. The retaining wall of the reservoir is concealed behind a grassy embankment. Also in the old days, there used to be a maintenance depot for the Navigations Company long before the formation of British Waterways.

The BCN is a much-loved system of canals, but it has to be said that some boaters are often put off from exploring them on their own. Sometimes it is simply rumours of problems, and it must be admitted that occasionally these turn out to be true. It may be just that one unused section may suffer from a lack of dredging. Shallow water and excessive weed growth prompt regular visits to the weed hatch, or even something worse that has got stuck around the prop. Also, on urban canals there is always the perception of trouble from louts, so our boating companions felt much safer in the small convoy.

After continuing for some time on the broad expanse of the Main Line Canal, we arrived at the oddly named Pudding Green Junction, West Bromwich, and proceeded another half mile to Ryder's Green Junction. We were now really entering the back waters of the BCN. This particular section of waterway is now known as the Walsall Canal, but in the early days it was in fact the first Midlands canal to be built, and was called the Wednesbury Canal. It opened in 1769. Sadly, much of the Wednesbury Old Canal has gone, and what is left has been cut in two by the new spine road. The final section, of around half a mile, is now the preserve of anglers and walkers, while boaters can still do the first half up to the Ridgeacre pub, and then wind to come back.

First, a word of caution. It is good to see a boat or two come up this old arm from time to time; and several canal guides depict a good channel with towpath. Unfortunately, the silt is so contaminated with toxic substances, that on past occasions

Entering the Oozells Loop to Sherborne Wharf.

when many boats went up the arm, the result was that all the fish were killed. So, my advice is moor at Ryder's Green Junction and walk the old canal. It has a good towpath and you will be back in no time.

Anyway, getting back to our cruise, we let narrowboat *Yorky* and a Wilderness boat test out the arm, while Brian, Brenda and myself went for a stroll with the dog after picking some fabulous blackberries at the junction. As soon as we arrived at Hadley Bridge, Phoenix Street, the sky went dark and the rain came down in torrents. This was not as bad as it sounded, for it gave us the opportunity to examine the bridge. Even to my untrained architectural eye it was obvious that the bridge had been formed in two stages.

Above: The Icknield Port Loop.

Left: Hadley Bridge on the Wednesbury Old Canal.

The original central bridge, constructed in either the late eighteenth or early nineteenth century, was of a different type of brick and just wide enough to take a horse and cart. It was widened in the middle of the nineteenth century, and a carved key stone gave the date of 1868. I would like to point out that there are very few structures left of this vintage. The little red fire doors still had their rollers on this bridge – they assisted the lowering and raising of the firemen's hoses into the canal.

Finally the rain stopped, the sun came out, and the little gathering of boats at the top of the Ryder's Green Junction set off down The Eight Locks. In one respect it was like the old days, to view a group of boats waiting their turn at the top lock. We noticed at this point that The Eight Lock's pub was closed down. This closing down of pubs is a recent phenomenon, brought about by a host of social, political and financial forces. One local newspaper stated that at least one pub a week was closing down in Sandwell. Now I am no great frequenter of pubs, but as they close, and then later get knocked down, it seems to be changing the nature of the Black Country. Besides, how do you give people directions? Forty years ago, the local pub was the life of the community; not any more.

Venturing along the remaining length of the WOC.

Above: Boats gather to go down the Ryder's Green Flight.

Left: Yorkie on the way down the Ryder's Green Flight.

The BCN cruisers stayed that night at Ocker Hill, before going on to boat much of the BCN, including the Wyrley & Essington, Cannock Extension Canal and also the infrequently boated Rushall Canal, before returning to the Main Line via the Tame Valley. For an August day it was amazingly cold, so Brenda popped into the galley and made a herbal tea. She tried hard to convince me that it was lemon balm, but honestly it was exactly the colour of canal water. So if she ever offers you a drink, be careful!

16

DUDLEY CANAL CELEBRATIONS, AUGUST 2008

One has to be careful with celebrations. A recently published book revealed that, in one year alone, almost two dozen people were killed by champagne corks, mostly at weddings. So, with that in mind, I and many more canal enthusiasts were cautiously looking forward to the celebrations on the Dudley Canal in August 2008. At this point, I would like to thank Paddy Grice and his wife; Steve Bingham, and all the other volunteers that worked so hard to make a great day at Netherton.

The big feature was, of course, the remembrance of the opening of the Netherton Tunnel, but other improvements of that same year – 1858 – included a rebuild to the Delph Locks, a cut across the canal at Bumble Hole, the opening out of Brewin's tunnel (a short tunnel near Netherton Reservoir), and the introduction of the Two Lock Line (another short cut near Merry Hill, now long gone).

So, on 20 August, we were treated to ribbon cuttings by local Mayors, Brass Bands, boat trips through the Dudley and Netherton Tunnels, a horse-boat, and a cavalcade of boats. When I looked up cavalcade in my dictionary, it said a procession of horses, but in this case it was actually boats. The BCNS were on hand, with others, to take a magnificent procession of boats, new and old, through the Netherton. But, and it is a big but, it all may never have happened.

The Netherton, though remarkable in many ways, has had its fair share of problems, and its future continues to hang in the balance. As soon as the tunnel was opened to traffic, problems were noticed when the bottom of the canal, the brick invert, heaved. This was due to geology, and not to the craftsmanship of the tunnel builders and designers.

The tunnel, as it passes under the Rowley Hills above, goes through a variety of strata. Some of it is hard rock; if it had all been hard rock then the build would have taken more time, but the end result would have been better. Unfortunately, the tunnel also passed through coal measures, and you know what the Black Country folk were like for digging that stuff away and to hell with the consequences. However, the worst substance was a soft blue clay-type material that the original engineers called blue bind (marl). Oh, it was much easier to dig, but when left to itself under that hillside, the pressures increased tremendously.

The bricks, both blue and brown, used on the tunnel – just over 26.5 million of them – were tested for their hardness. However, there is nothing like time and high pressure to ruin a decent brick. The British Waterways guys call it spalling; the way that a brick, will, over time, crack and then turn to dust. There is evidence of some spalling going on in the tunnel, not just under the water but in the side walls and crown.

THE PRINCIPAL INSPECTION

So, every month British Waterways send one of their chaps through the tunnel looking for problems, and then every three years they do what is called a principal inspection. This is essentially a detailed study of everything, yard by yard. The last time they took a boat through, they also used an LED attached to a laptop to look down the seven remaining air shafts.

When I was a child, one of the most exciting things I ever did was go through the Netherton Tunnel. It was a kind of dare in those days, and if you could not make it then you were branded a 'chicken'. We thought that those shafts were for ventilation. Well, I suppose that is what they were left for. In the beginning though, they were part of the construction method.

For the Netherton, seventeen shafts were dug until the excavators reached the right depth. Then the tunnellers went in, both directions, from the bottom of each shaft. This method ensured that the tunnel was finished, right up to the last brick in two years and seven months. That was a tremendous feat with the technology of the time.

The principal inspection has revealed that there is always a bit of movement going on down there, but do not be alarmed, at the moment it is fine. Boaters have unrestricted movement both ways through the tunnel, though walkers are directed to use the east towpath, as there are a lot of potholes and problems on the other side. When bricks are found to be spalling, the contractors come along and use a type of spray concrete, reinforced with fibres. This does not look nearly as attractive as the original brickwork, but sometimes the perfect remedy is not always possible – or affordable.

Actually, when we went through, much of the brickwork was seen to be in remarkably good condition. At a few locations though, helical ties have been used to strengthen the brickwork. This kind of work was also utilised recently on the Steward Aqueduct, not too far from the tunnel. Holes are drilled through the brickwork and long metal rods are glued within, thus tying everything together for many more years.

The bed of the canal also has to be inspected, because this is where most of the problems have come from. The inspectors carefully measure the depth of water, down to the cinders and puddle that line the bottom of the canal. If the measurements are short then they know they have a problem.

So now you know why I started off by talking about death by champagne corks, but let us look on the bright side. The Netherton Tunnel is a jewel in the crown of the

Above: Bob Price –Mayor of Sandwell, Pat Martin Deputy Mayor of Dudley, and other dignitaries at the northern end of the tunnel in 2008.

Left: Paddy Grice, prime organiser of the DCT Celebrations.

On board *Electra*, and ready for the trip through the tunnel.

Inside the Netherton tunnel of 1858 vintage.

All safe at Bumble Hole, Netherton.

BCN, and is an important and exciting part of many trips throughout the Midlands. At the August celebrations, we were thrilled to have a horse-boat as part of the ensemble. This reminded me of an incident told to me by an old horse-boater some years ago.

One day, he came to the mouth of the tunnel, as he had for some years, only this time he had a new horse to break in. Well, when he got to the mouth of the tunnel the horse became increasingly frightened; and after only a few hundred yards the animal went out of control and into the canal. Only after much exhausting effort did they manage to get the poor creature out of the water. So, what did our determined boatman do? He simply put a piece of sacking over the horse's eyes, and led him back through the tunnel – no more problems. The moral of this story is, if you have someone in you boat party that gets scared, put a paper bag over their head before they go into the depths – that will do the trick.

As we boated serenely through the tunnel, with powerful lamps flashing around the brickwork, we had a debate about the handrail. No one seems to know definitely whether there was a handrail right from the beginning. If there was, then this would have meant that the tow rope from the horse would have rubbed tightly over the rail from one end to the other. It is equally difficult, however, to imagine leading a horse through the tunnel without the support of a rail, even though it was lit by gas. If you know for definite, one way or the other, please let me know.

As for me, I have just one gripe, and that is to do with the tunnel measurements. In the old days, the tunnel used to announce proudly on a small plaque affixed to the entrance portal, 'Netherton Tunnel 3,027 Yards'. That little piece of history was removed some years ago and replaced with a new sign, '2,776 Metres'. Now, I ask you, what does 2,776 metres signify? 3,027 yards looks and sounds so right, 2,776, does not look like anything really. Oddly enough, when I was researching the original documents they said that the tunnel was 3,036 yards – but I am certainly not about to get my 10-yard tape measure out and go and check it!

Other titles published by The History Press

BOATS, SMOKE, STEAM AND FOLK
EXPLORING THE CANALS OF THE WEST MIDLANDS

Robert Davies

Over a period of fifty or so years a network of canals and inland waterways connecte
Britain's major towns and industrial centres. Exploring the canals of the Midlands, thi
book, with maps and detailed walks, will encourage the reader to move from his armchai
and into this living piece of history. It also includes interviews and memories of those wh
worked on the canals.

978 0 7524 1765 3

MIDLANDS CANALS
MEMORIES OF THE CANAL CARRIERS

Robert Davies

This superbly researched and illustrated book is a compilation of interviews with a handfu
of the folk who worked the canals during the final decades of commercial canal carrying
and captures the flavour of this lost era. Among those interviewed are those that regularly
travelled the narrow canals from the Midlands industrial region down to London, and from
the Midlands north to Manchester and Runcorn.

978 0 7524 3910 5

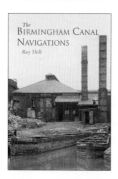

THE BIRMINGHAM CANAL NAVIGATIONS
Ray Shill

The Birmingham Canal Navigations lie at the heart of the British canal network and hav
a rich heritage that spans over two centuries. The BCN network developed over a perio
of one hundred years and served the busiest and most concentrated industrial region o
the country – earning Birmingham the nickname of 'Little Venice'. Ray Shill examines th
industrial archaeology of the network, looking at the structures, trade, work and craft o
the waterway, as well as providing detailed maps of the network's various sections.

978 0 7524 2767 9

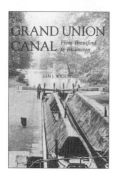

THE GRAND UNION CANAL
FROM BRENTFORD TO BRAUNSTON

Ian J. Wilson

Leaving the River Thames at Brentford and travelling through the Home Counties
to Birmingham and Leicester, the Grand Union Canal wends its way through sylvan
countryside and market towns on its route from London to the Midlands. Using antique
postcards and photographs to illustrate the story, Ian J. Wilson tells of the group of canals
that came together to form the Grand Union Canal.

978 0 7524 2933 5

Visit our website and discover thousands of other History Press books.

www.thehistorypress.co.uk